RECOVERY
from
SMOKING

About the book

Proven methods to stop smoking and find the freedom of recovery are presented in down-to-earth, gentle, and supportive language by Elizabeth Hanson Hoffman, Ph.D., who quit smoking using these methods. Anybody who wants to quit smoking can get solid help here. Try the exercises and slowly, patiently work your way to healthy living. Professionals and others who work with people in treatment for alcoholism and other addictions will also find much valuable information. They can use it to help the large population of recovering alcoholics and others who want to heal from the disease of smoking.

About the authors

Elizabeth Hanson Hoffman, Ph.D., is a recovering nicotine addict with a private practice as a clinical psychologist. She conducts recovery programs on nicotine cessation and offers other therapies. Her expertise includes treatment of chemical dependency and codependency. She has been on numerous radio and television shows. Her articles have appeared in newspapers and health-related publications.

Despite her knowledge and experience, which could have helped her to quit, the author was able to stop smoking only through combining psychology with a Twelve Step approach.

Christopher Douglas Hoffman, L.S.W., A.C.S.W., is a social worker in private practice and recovering nicotine addict. He provides counseling and consulting services to individuals and industry, with a special interest in nicotine dependency services. Mr. Hoffman conducts outpatient treatment services for nicotine addicts and is actively involved in community-based initiatives to address the problem of adolescent smoking.

RECOVERY *from* SMOKING

Quitting with the Twelve Step Process

Second Edition
Updated and Revised

Elizabeth Hanson Hoffman, Ph.D.
Christopher Douglas Hoffman, L.S.W., A.C.S.W.

HAZELDEN

Hazelden
Center City, Minnesota 55012-0176
1-800-328-0094
1-651-257-1331 (FAX).
www.hazelden.org

ISBN: 1-56838-307-X
Library of Congress Catalog Card Number: 91-72848
Printed in the United States of America.

Credits:
Excerpt from MANY ROADS, ONE JOURNEY by Charlotte Davis Kasl, Copyright
© 1991, Charlotte Davis Kasl. Reprinted by arrangement with HarperCollins
Publishers and the author.
    Excerpts from WOMEN, SEX, AND ADDICTION: A SEARCH FOR LOVE AND
POWER by Charlotte Kasl. Copyright © 1989 by Charlotte Kasl. Reprinted by per-
mission of Ticknor & Fields, a Houghton Mifflin Co., and the author.
    All (family) roles originally published in *The Family Trap*, 1976 © by Sharon
Wegscheider-Cruse. Also published in *Choicemaking*, 1986 © by Sharon
Wegscheider-Cruse, Health Communications. Reprinted by permission of Health
Communications and the author.
    Core issues originally published in *Healing the Child Within*, 1987 (p. 196)
© by Charles L. Whitfield, Health Communications. Also published in *Synopsis
of Co-dependence*, 1991, © by Charles L. Whitfield, Health Communications. Reprinted by permission of Health Communications and the author.
    Compulsive behaviors originally published in *A Gift to Myself*, 1990 (p. 45) ©
by Charles L. Whitfield, Health Communications. Reprinted by permission of
Health Communications and the author.
    The Twelve Steps and Twelve Traditions are reprinted and adapted with the
permission of Alcoholics Anonymous. Permission to reprint and adapt does not
mean that A.A. has reviewed or approved the contents of this publication, nor
that A.A. agrees with the views expressed herein.
    The Serenity Prayer for Smokers and *The Twelve Promises* are copyrighted 1988 by
Nicotine Anonymous World Services, San Francisco. *Tips for Gaining Freedom from
Nicotine* © 1989 by Nicotine Anonymous World Services. All are reprinted with
the generous permission of Nicotine Anonymous World Services.

To Rusty, Chris, Elizabeth, and Henry:
You are my greatest joy.
Also to my parents:
I love you and miss you.

Contents

Acknowledgments

AS I RE-READ this book, I was amazed at how many people helped me in my recovery. Some of the authors and teachers who shared their research and insights are cited in this book, others are not. Many people have touched my life, and I couldn't possibly credit each thought and word to the original source. I appreciate the collective wisdom of all these named and unnamed people.

Everyone who read the manuscript during its various stages of completion gave me valuable feedback. I thank Patrick Carnes, Ellen Danfield, Sarah Sandberg Fischer, Susan Gilius, Rusty Hanson, Henry Hanson, Christopher Hoffman, Charlotte Kasl, Hanne Kulin, Kathleen Parsons, Jeff Pincus, Nancy Risser, Max Schneider, Ann Smith, Diane Teske, Eugene York, Merritt Wallick, Todd Witmer, and David Wilderman.

Carol Clellan, Lois Dunnevant, Siri Neel Singh Khalsa, and Lydia Spivey also contributed. Beth Hoffman and Lisa Paponetti assisted in manuscript research. Naeya Bowen, Jamie Stover, Henry Troup, and Bonnie Wildeman helped in preparation of the manuscript. I thank all of you.

Sharon Wegscheider-Cruse, Charlotte Kasl, and Charles Whitfield permitted me to use portions of their material in this book, as did Alcoholics Anonymous and Nicotine Anonymous. I appreciate this support and cooperation.

I am grateful to Silvan Tomkins for his friendship and support. To all my mentors and teachers, I say thank you. Much of your training and insight became evident to me as I worked on this project.

I want to acknowledge, with appreciation and respect, how much I have learned from my clients. Each day I learn something new from the process and unfolding of your recovery. I am privileged to be a part of it.

Acknowledgments

Uncle Bob and Aunt Barbie, you have been consistently nurturing and supportive to me. Hank, you encouraged this project from the very first draft. Rusty, your gentle firmness in addressing my nicotine addiction was crucial to my recovery. My friends and support system have been enthusiastic and helpful to me during my writing of this book. I thank each one of you. Doug, I appreciate your years of encouragement and support, too.

For my children, Chris and Elizabeth, and my closest friend, Henry Troup, I feel very grateful. With all the work that went into each of our lives in this past year, we still had time for many wonderful talks, much tenderness, and a healthy share of fun and laughter.

I acknowledge my appreciation for the enthusiasm and support of Hazelden for this project. My editors, Tim McIndoo and Karen Chernyaev, patiently worked many hours to make this book possible. I appreciate their belief in the project and their feedback. Thank you, Tim and Karen.

I give special thanks to my son, Chris, for his intelligent assistance in this revised edition. Since the book's first edition, Chris has become an insightful and competent psychotherapist and has joined me in private practice. My research and corporate consulting is easier and much more fun because of his energy, perspective, and enthusiasm. Chris is also a recovering nicotine addict. We share the awe and gratitude for the gifts of nicotine recovery, in both our personal and professional lives. Thank you, Chris, for being exactly who you are!

Introduction

I AM A RECOVERING nicotine addict and nicotine addicts are hooked. The drug is powerful, mood-altering. It can pep us up or calm us down, depending on how deeply we inhale and how many puffs we take. Nicotine can improve concentration, help us cope with stress, and suppress our feelings so we can appear to be in control. We can light up and retreat into our own little world as we get our fix. The rituals of smoking provide security and comfort in an unpredictable world. No wonder the drug is addictive!

The apparent benefits fade quickly as we grow more addicted, losing touch with ourselves not only physically but also emotionally and spiritually. *Euphoric recall* (remembering the "good times") tells us that smoking makes us feel better. But as soon as we light up we feel worse and wonder why we keep doing this to ourselves. The disease gets bigger and bigger, and everything else in our life gets smaller. Before we hit bottom, our denial and our minimizing tell us *I'm not that bad, yet. I'll stop before I get that bad. Everyone dies of something. This is one of my few vices.* Some of us don't live long enough to hit bottom. We keep smoking until it kills us. Like alcoholism, the disease of nicotine addiction is "cunning, baffling, powerful."[*]

I am a recovering nicotine addict who believes that sharing my experience, strength, and hope with other addicts will help keep me from picking up a cigarette, one day at a time. Part I, "My Story," is intensely personal so you can see what *my* life was like in the grips of my addiction and what it's like today. You will see clearly that my academic training and professional insight alone were not enough to deal with my addiction.

---

[*] From "How It Works," *Alcoholics Anonymous*, 3rd ed., New York: Alcoholics Anonymous World Services Inc., 1976, 58–59.

Introduction

Besides being a nicotine addict, I am a psychologist who specializes in addiction and codependency. This perspective contributes to Part II, "Your Story." Its chapters provide information and exercises to help you in your physical, emotional, and spiritual recovery. I describe a Twelve Step approach called Nicotine Anonymous, which I believe is essential to recovery from nicotine addiction. Materials are included to help you start your own support group, according to the Steps and Traditions adapted from Alcoholics Anonymous.

Although these chapters emphasize *your* story, I have commented on how these areas affected me. The most valuable input early in my recovery came from other recovering nicotine addicts. (It takes one to know one.)

Using this Book to Your Best Advantage

I use the self-help approach. First, we need to be aware of how much nicotine controls our life and we need to assess that influence carefully. Once we decide to recover, it is important to explore old knowledge and reprogram ourselves to break the cycle.

My graduate school training in psychology was in cognitive behavioral therapy. This simply means that I learned how to help people change what they think and how they behave. I include many exercises in this book to help you change the way you think and behave as you recover from nicotine addiction. You may want to buy a notebook to write down your answers and keep this information in one place.

Breaking the Cycle

Learning to identify and express feelings in a healthy way is very important in recovery. Also, recovering people often find it helpful to develop their spirituality. This book contains guidelines for dealing with these parts of being human (emotions and spirit). New thoughts and behavior are suggested to help you cope more effectively without smoking.

To break cycles we first have to be aware of them. This often means going back and looking at our family of origin to discover clues about how these cycles began and why they were maintained. This approach is common in treating codependency and in the Adult Children of Alcoholics movement. It is valuable to connect the "then" of our life to the "here and now" and to make choices about what we want to maintain and what we want to change.

Change Is a Process

Recently there has been some interesting research focusing on how people make a major change in life, such as quitting smoking. The findings indicate that there are several stages that someone goes through in this process of change. The process actually begins before a smoker decides he or she even wants to quit. A person then moves in stages through setting a quit date, quitting, and entering a life of recovery from smoking. This process may be quick for some and take longer for others. A person's goal at each of the stages of change is to get to the next stage. If you are at the very beginning of this process, and have not decided that you want to quit, a reasonable goal may be that when you reach the end of this book you will have made a decision. If you do wish to quit, but have not been able to set a quit date and stick to it, a reasonable goal is to set a quit date that you can manage. If you have a quit date set, your goal might be to get involved in a Twelve Step group and learn new skills you will need to not pick up a cigarette, one day at a time. If you have quit, a goal might be to continue to practice new recovery skills, and seek support in the Twelve-Step community. The most important thing to remember is that *everyone* is in the process of change; by reading this book you will be adding the skills needed to move you toward recovery. As you progress, remember the following: Be gentle with yourself, because addiction is about abuse, and recovery is about healing. Take your time, because we each move at our own pace. Seek support, because we don't have to do this alone.

Slowing Down with Fresh Air, not Smoke

Nicotine addicts are notorious for being in a rush! It's hard for us to sit down and take the time to develop honest insight about ourselves. We are too busy rushing around, trying to figure out everything else. Scientific research tells us that writing about our thoughts and feelings increases awareness and helps us change our behavior. Years ago *Recovery from Smoking* started as a journal in which I recorded my struggle to stop smoking.

Since it is a challenge to devote time to our recovery, I want to talk about how to use this book. Please do not try to read it in one weekend. Rather, take your time. Be systematic about completing the exercises. After you complete a few, take a break and talk about your insights with someone who is interested in your recovery. In essence, read this book at a slow and steady pace.

As smokers we need to learn to slow down and to relax by taking a deep breath of fresh air, not smoke. Usually we take shallow breaths unless we are inhaling deeply to get our fix. Recovering smokers often think of reaching for a cigarette when what our body is really telling us is, *Slow down. Take a deep breath.* One of the things I missed most when I stopped smoking was inhaling deeply. Often I had to remind myself that even though I wasn't smoking, I could still take a deep breath—of fresh air.

My emotional and spiritual progress have come from pushing aside the busyness to allow open space. With reflection I become receptive to insight and inspiration. In these moments inner wisdom fills the empty spaces and I know I am connecting with a "higher power." The written exercises in this book are guides to insight and inspiration, but we need to quiet the busyness to get their full value. We need to slow down and take a deep breath.

Establishing New Habits

Old habits die hard; new habits require practice. Before each exercise, I remind you to slow down and take time for your recovery. I ask you to

Remember to *stop*.
Take three slow, deep breaths. *
Take your time as you complete the exercise.

At several points I ask you to stop for another reason: Insight that comes from the exercises is important, but it won't take us far if we don't follow it with action. With no change in behavior,

---

* Breathing exercise: (1) Place a hand on your abdomen. (2) Expand your abdomen as you inhale slowly to the count of four. (3) Hold your breath to the count of two. (4) Exhale slowly to the count of four, contracting your abdomen. (5) Repeat these steps three times.

insight leaves us feeling frustrated and guilty. Periodically we need to stop and ask ourselves, *What am I willing to do today for my recovery?*

In my active nicotine addiction I was not aware of my feelings and needs. I was far more focused on how others saw me than on how I saw myself. I also paid more attention to the feelings, needs, and behavior of others than to my own. This problem is often called *codependency*. I agree with the researchers who believe that codependency underlies most addiction. In my recovery from addiction I had to become aware of *my* feelings and needs, or I suspect I would have started smoking again. Therefore, this book offers many exercises to help heal the codependency.

As I write these words I am a grateful recovering nicotine addict who hasn't smoked a cigarette, one day at a time, since March 22, 1987. I hope reading this book helps you as much as writing it has helped me.

New Research

After the first edition of this book was published in 1991, it became the manual for a nicotine treatment program at the Caron Foundation in Wernersville, Pennsylvania. We found excellent long-term nicotine abstinence results.[2] The program teaches smokers how to cope with life and handle feelings so they can stay smoke free. We also found that using Twelve Step support is crucial.

This revised edition contains the book's original material, which has demonstrated effectiveness, combined with new tips and research so we may all continue our progress in *Recovery from Smoking: Quitting with the 12 Step Process.*

PART I: *My Story*

CHAPTER 1

A Physical, Emotional, And Spiritual Disease

HI. MY NAME IS LIZ and I'm a psychologist, mother of two children, and a recovering nicotine addict. For twenty-seven years my relationship with nicotine was the most important relationship in my life. When I was active in my addiction I appeared to be successful, but I lived a double life. This is the story of what living in the prison of addiction was like for me, what has happened so far in my recovery, and what my life is like today.

I started smoking at age thirteen. It seemed like such a grown-up thing to do. At sixteen I drove around in my 1952 Buick Special, smoking cigarettes and laughing with my friends. At school I would go to my car after lunch to smoke with friends before afternoon classes. I remember one day when we sat smoking in my car, joking about our immature classmates who were meeting in the gym to plan a pep rally. We were far more sophisticated than they. This was really living!

I smoked throughout my twenties and early thirties. I felt a buzz most of the time in the early stages of my addiction. Although physical problems had started to develop, I denied them and did not associate any of them with smoking. I remember taking a deep breath in bed one night and feeling my feet get numb. I ate very little food. I seemed to need only cigarettes and coffee. I remember feeling proud when others would comment about how skinny I was.

By my late thirties I was obsessed with smoking. (Should I quit? Could I quit? How could I quit? Was I dying? Was it my fault?) I felt sick most of the time, often with an upset stomach. I had constant coughs and sinus headaches. (I must have cleared my throat a hundred times a day.) I carried cough drops, Extra-Strength Sinutabs, and Tums with me faithfully. This is what feeling "normal" meant to me. I didn't know it wasn't normal until after I stopped smoking, when my upset stomach, head-aches, and cough went away. And the obsession stopped, too.

The Insanity

I went to extraordinary lengths to keep the drug nicotine in my body. Such memories bring me sadness and shame, but I need to remember how low I sank in my addiction and how clearly denial kept me from seeing the insanity of my lifestyle. There were many instances of that insanity. I want to share a few examples with you.

I smoked during both of my pregnancies. I asked other nico-tine addicts if I should quit. They confirmed my belief: to quit during pregnancy would be traumatic for the baby. We all agreed it would be better to keep smoking. Today I know this was not the truth. It was denial and addiction talking.

I remember being hospitalized for five days with a collapsed lung. I did not respond to normal treatments—there was too little elasticity in my lung—so I required special treatments. I remember lighting cigarettes between those treatments and watching the smoke swirl around the tubes attached to my body. Never did it occur to me to stop smoking. People say addiction is the disease of denial. I can vouch for that. In the hospital I was surrounded by friends (nicotine addicts, of course). They would stand lookout for the doctors so I could snuff my cigarette before my doctor could catch me smoking. What fun we thought it was to avoid detection. Nicotine addiction is "cunning, baffling, powerful," and we were a sick crew.

Several years later, I spent over a month frequently visiting a family member with advanced emphysema in the intensive care unit of a local hospital. She was kept alive by a respirator. In the waiting room I'd smoke constantly until it was time to visit her again. After weeks of struggle, she turned off her respirator as the nurses looked the other way. She finally found peace as her struggle for breath ceased. The first thing I did when I heard the news of her death was to reach for a cigarette to calm my nerves. Obviously, I couldn't stop smoking then; I was too upset! In fact, I smoked more than ever. It was insane, I see that today. No doubt about it: Nicotine causes insanity.

Cigarettes were the first thing I cared about in the morning and the last thing I cared about at night. Nothing could stop me from keeping a supply in the house. I went to convenience stores late at night, drove on icy roads, and spent my last penny if necessary. I smoked in front of my children, even though it scared them. I continued smoking, even though it scared me that I would die from my addiction: physical symptoms were evident—for example, shortness of breath, chest pain, coughing, circulatory problems. If that's not insanity, I don't know what is!

Emotional Shambles

Emotionally my life was in shambles. I was snapping in and out of withdrawal. My mood depended on the level of nicotine in my bloodstream. I often thought about dying of cancer and heart disease. I was scared the doctors who referred clients to me would discover that I smoked and I would lose credibility. I felt like a fraud, hiding my smoking from people who would be amazed that I had such a "stupid" habit. After all, I was a psychologist who worked with addictions. Certainly I should be able to stop smoking. "Physician, heal thyself," goes the saying. Well, I didn't know myself, and I couldn't heal myself while I was still active in my addiction!

Constantly I felt afraid and had a sense of urgency. Today I know that nicotine often affects people that way. When I smoked I believed the fear was real and meant impending doom. I believed the urgency meant I had to accomplish more and do it faster. I had no concept of serenity or peace. To me, tranquility was only the name of a sea on the moon, not a state of being.

The last few years of my addiction I felt too ashamed and guilty to smoke around most people. I became increasingly isolated. Toward the end of my smoking I would typically come home from work with a project as an excuse to isolate myself. I'd close myself off in a room and smoke as much as I possibly could. I smoked until I could hardly breathe. Then I would drag myself to my bedroom, vowing, *I'll quit in the morning.* Before I prepared for bed I would douse the remaining cigarettes with water (if I hadn't smoked them all). And then, ceremoniously, I'd throw away the pack with well-chosen words of disgust and self-loathing.

I'd awaken in the middle of the night with sharp chest pains. They were so severe that I had to hold my breath until the pain passed. Of course, I couldn't ask a doctor about them because I would expose myself as a heavy smoker who could not stop, even in the face of severe pain. I felt like such a "bad" person: a truly deficient human being.

After this horror, I would awaken the next morning hungover with chest pain and a foul-tasting mouth, vowing, No *more*. If not that day, then that evening for sure, I would shut myself away and start this ritual of late-stage addiction all over again.

I really wanted to stop smoking at this point, but I didn't believe I could. I reasoned that even if I could stop briefly, I'd think about cigarettes constantly and begin eating continuously and gain a lot of weight. Then I would be an obsessed, obese nicotine addict who had to start smoking again to lose the weight. So why bother stopping? It made perfect sense to me. The disease of nicotine addiction was talking, and I believed it completely.

I used nicotine in a precise way to control my feelings. I could regulate its intake by the size of the puff and by the nicotine count of the brand. Any intensity of feeling that I experienced was a cue to smoke a cigarette. Because I started smoking at age thirteen, I hadn't experienced nonmedicated feelings for many years! People said talking to me was like talking to a computer: I was so "logical." The truth is that I really couldn't feel many of my feelings. As a psychologist, this was a considerable handicap.

All my feelings were affected by nicotine—even the positive ones. My happiness was always, somehow, mixed up with a sense of being hyper. Happiness was more an excitement or a wired sensation, not the joy and contentment that comes from a sense of well-being. (Nicotine, I have learned, is too much of a stimulant for that.) I often confused the feeling I got when receiving my fix: I called it "relaxation" and "happiness," when it was only the cessation of withdrawal feelings that I had experienced a minute earlier.

Actually I was afraid of feeling my feelings. I was afraid they would be too intense. But this glimpse of intensity was just the withdrawal between cigarettes. When I was active in my addiction, my emotional life was in shambles. Nicotine had me in its grasp: mind, body, and soul.

Spirituality

When I was five years old I had frequent nightmares. I dreamed I was riding in a little red car that drove over a cliff. I knew that when the car hit bottom, I'd be dead. I also knew that I had to believe in God before I died. As I was falling off the cliff, the pressure was intense to become a believer. Night after night, in this scary dream, I would try so hard to believe in God before hitting bottom. But I couldn't convince myself during the fall and I would awaken, crying out in fear. Mother comforted me, and Daddy assured me that I could believe in God.

I didn't think much more about God until I was eight years old. My grandmother, whom I adored, suddenly became ill. For the first time in my life, I prayed to God for a favor. I asked that my grandmother get well. Yet it seemed she died almost immediately after my prayer. Either God didn't exist or he was a very scary guy. Whichever it was, I decided not to ask him for any more help. My relationship with God faded and my strategy changed.

Science or Religion?

In high school and college I began to read philosophy. By then I smoked heavily. I remember feeling afraid and hyper most of the time, as if I were about to lose control. I lived on coffee and cigarettes for years, searching for peace and safety by reading philosophy. I thought my search was for understanding and mastery (control) over my life. Since I couldn't depend on God to help, it was up to me to take care of myself.

As I advanced in college, my approach became scientific. In my arrogance, I believed science was going to answer all my questions about predictability and control. I'd be safe at last! In my statistics class, "God" became *unexplained variance*. It seemed to me that as we understood more through scientific methodology, we attributed less to God. The uneducated and superstitious might always need God as an answer to stop all further questions, but I would not join the crowd that used God as a cop-out, an aspirin to kill pain. Arrogance and grandiosity are important parts of addiction, and I had my share.

Shortly before my dad died, I seriously wondered: *When my father dies, will I find God through a religious experience?* I noticed that only people in crisis seemed to have the religious experience of finding God. I wondered if my dad's death would be enough of a crisis for this to happen to me. At the time, I was afraid that since I "knew" how the process occurred, this knowledge would somehow interfere with the naive approach that was necessary for me to have a religious experience.

I didn't learn until much later that I can intentionally suspend my logic and rationality in order to become quiet and listen to that other, noncognitive, part of me. At that time, all I knew was that I probably couldn't get it, whatever "it" was. I had many books and scientific publications but no serenity or peace of mind. I had plenty of cigarettes, however, and I smoked away as I tried in vain to figure it all out.

One year after my dad died, my mother died. I was devastated. I had exhausted all my energy in trying to figure out the answers. I still didn't have any clue about the existence of God, but I did have my first spiritual awakening: I surrendered. On an intellectual and emotional level, I gave up my quest for the truth. Whatever the "truth" was seemed fine to me because that's just the way it was! For me, truth had come to mean *what is,* and I finally realized that I didn't have to understand it.

Surrender

This surrender was quiet and calm. I felt still and safe. There were no fireworks or histrionics, just peace. I realized that I can safely surrender to what "is" with awe, without having to understand, explain, or control in any way.

"The Serenity Prayer" by Reinhold Niebuhr became a large part of my new spiritual life.

> *God grant me the serenity*
> *To accept the things I cannot change,*
> *The courage to change the things I can,*
> *And the wisdom to know the difference.*

I was amazed to realize that most things I'd worried about (what happened in the past, what other people say and do, what others may say and do in the future) fell into the category of "things I can't change." My job is to accept, as reality, everything I cannot change. That's simple. Accepting reality, instead of resisting it, frees up much time to change the things I can (such as my attitudes, my thoughts, and my behavior).

Part of accepting reality was learning how to deal with my family. In this process, I had experiences that showed me that (a) certainly *I* was not in charge of the grand plan; and (b) although it seems that some pattern or power is responsible for life's order, I didn't have to figure it all out. To my amazement, when I stopped trying to fix and control the lives of others, I started focusing on the things I could change, like dealing more effectively with my smoking.

Kicking the Habit

I tried many approaches to stop smoking.

- acupuncture
- Bach remedies
- filters
- going to health retreats
- hypnosis
- increasing physical exercise
- limiting the cigarettes smoked
- listening to subliminal tapes
- Nicorette gum
- reading inspirational books
- SmokeEnders
- smoking only in certain places at certain times
- switching to lower-tar cigarettes

I tried these and many other clever devices. I expected something magic to happen to me so I wouldn't have to say no to the disease that says "just one won't hurt."

I heard colleagues say that active nicotine addiction prevents us from sensitively identifying and expressing feelings. I wanted to experience my unmedicated feelings. I knew I needed to stop smoking and I was struggling. I still believed I had to do it alone. The words *nicotine addiction* were still just words to me. I had not yet surrendered to the fact that I was addicted and needed help from others.

In 1986 I wrote in a journal, "The Smoking Papers," which reflects my struggle. In these few entries, you will note that I was able to "white-knuckle" it for a couple of weeks. Then I fell back into the addiction and stayed there until I put together a support system of other nicotine addicts.

My Story

May 28, 1986. I am tired of the broken promises with regard to cigarette smoking. I am making a conscious effort today. It's really hard, I want to smoke. It would be so easy to pick up a cigarette, but I would feel so bad. My mouth would burn and the gross taste would stay all day. I will not smoke now.

May 29, 1986. Today has been another disappointment: three cigarettes and little motivation. I am working on an optimistic attitude. I need to work on self-restraint. I will not smoke today.

May 29, 1986. That was what I thought earlier. I smoked. I feel like such a failure. I feel so guilty. I have two wonderful children, a nice home, and a rewarding career, and I continue to smoke. I am really struggling.

June 2, 1986. First day back on track. Today I threw away all the cigarettes and lighters. Time to stop the self-pity, now just do it: don't smoke.

July 2, 1986. It's been a long time without a cigarette: June 19 was my first day as a nonsmoker. It's still new and I feel a little rocky, but I am grateful I haven't smoked. I think I can do this on my own.

July 5, 1986. I blew it again. After a meeting on Thursday night, I felt scared and angry and I smoked a cigarette. Self-pity started, then it magnified. Not just one cigarette but one pack. Self-pity and shame are all I can feel.

March 22, 1987. Finally I surrendered and "gave" my nicotine obsession to my Higher Power. (I hope s/he doesn't give it back!) I need to talk to Rusty and get support from other people who share the same problem. I tried it on my own last June, could only "white-knuckle" it for a few weeks, and couldn't enjoy all the benefits of a full recovery program. This time, I'm not going to do it alone. It doesn't work when I do. I'm going to ask for help. I need other recovering nicotine addicts! I don't have to stop smoking forever; I just have to not smoke "right now" and let the future up to my Higher Power.

What My Life Is Like Today

I am a nicotine addict who has not smoked since 1987, and I have only gained eight pounds. Today I don't obsess about smoking or crave cigarettes. I do think about them, however: when I see someone puffing away I feel grateful that I'm not chained to them anymore. I remember the hell of my smoking addiction, and I don't want to return.

Smoking is no longer the most important relationship in my life. I have many relationships today that I value. Freedom from the obsession is such a gift!

My journey has at times been intense and painful. I have been touched by the experiences and strength of other recovering addicts, and I have learned to listen to that gentle and loving voice that comes from deep inside.

I smoked cigarettes as a ritual to forget myself and get past my pain. I didn't want pain in my life. I dreaded situations I thought would be painful. I did everything I could to control my life to avoid pain. The pain mostly came from feelings I had buried for many years. These are the feelings I smoked over, to numb myself and to avoid facing pain.

As a therapist, I clearly recognized that I needed to stop smoking, feel the pain, and let it pass so I could grow emotionally and spiritually. My professional training taught me that the negative feelings pass quickly when they are acknowledged and accepted. When the pain passes, there is room for something else: joy and laughter.

I benefited greatly from moving through my painful feelings. They forced me to stretch my limits and look to others for guidance and support. Pain softened me and made me more empathetic toward other people. By accepting and moving through the pain, I gained new knowledge and awareness. I moved many steps along the path of enlightenment. I am grateful to have had such a worthwhile and exciting journey.

Today the Serenity Prayer is an important part of my life. I pray for the wisdom to know the difference between what I can and cannot change. Then I spend my time trying to change the things I can and working on accepting the things I can't change. It's simple, but not easy. It has made the biggest difference in my life.

Nicotine was my main coping mechanism for many years. I was missing the mark, but I was coping in the tradition of addiction and external "fixes." Healing my underlying codependency has helped me to avoid returning to cigarettes. Today my program of self-care includes daily exercise and meditation, a balance of work and leisure activities, and rewarding personal and professional relationships. No longer must I hide behind a smoke screen. My total program of recovery started with abstinence from nicotine. The way I feel today is the way I tried to feel all those years as I dragged on my cigarettes: peaceful and calm. I have a sense that I am who I am supposed to be, and I am doing what I'm supposed to be doing. I'm not living a life of addiction and secrets. This is the feeling of well-being that I searched for most of my life.

Today I am not a zealot or evangelist in my approach to not smoking. I don't try to reform anyone. If others are interested in my story, I share it. I emphasize that I am an addict who remembers the power of the disease. My recovery is not an accomplishment or achievement. It is truly a gift, a gift I never believed I'd receive: freedom from cigarettes and the obsession to smoke.

To stop smoking I needed the *desire* to stop smoking, the *willingness* to do "whatever it takes," and the honesty and commitment to work on a program of recovery one day at a time. Sounds like an outrageous series of requirements, doesn't it? Fortunately I didn't have to do it perfectly, or all at once, or alone. Progress, not perfection, is the strategy. Amazing physical, emotional, and spiritual rewards are the outcome.

Writing this story helps me. It helps me remember what my life was like when I was struggling with my addiction. I need to remember that my previous attempts to stop smoking didn't work because I had not accepted my life-threatening disease. I will never be cured, but I am grateful for remission! I am an addict. I am not like other people who can have just one. I am only *one* cigarette away from active addiction. My recovery depends on total abstinence, one day at a time, in combination with support from others and a connection with my Higher Power.

PART II: *Your Story*

CHAPTER 2

Physical Recovery

NICOTINE ADDICTION IS a worldwide epidemic.[1] In the United States it is the most common form of drug addiction and is responsible for 20 percent of all deaths. Forty-five percent of all smokers will die as a result of using tobacco.[2,3,4]

Nicotine addiction affects us physically, emotionally, and spiritually. Chapters 2, 3, and 4 give you a chance to examine the toll nicotine has taken on you and what can be done to turn your life around.

What is the average smoker's plight? Here are some signs of physical deterioration.

- a constant cough
- shortness of breath
- frequent colds
- sinus headaches
- upset stomach
- wrinkled skin
- a flabby body (from inactivity)
- foul-smelling hair and skin
- rotten breath
- stained fingers and teeth

The nicotine addict is *truly* not a glamorous or healthy human being!

Smoking is not just another bad habit. Nicotine is a powerful, addictive, mood-altering drug. This chapter addresses the issues of physical recovery—your physical recovery—in four parts. You will learn about (a) the physiology of addiction; (b) the process and benefits of quitting; (c) ways to minimize weight gain; and (d) an ongoing self-care program so you can develop and maintain better physical health.

The Physiology of Addiction

It was a lie. Smoking did not make me more sophisticated or mature, although it seemed my rite of passage into adulthood. I got hooked on the ritual: what helped kill my parents nearly destroyed me, too. My addiction progressed until I felt rotten all the time and was deeply ashamed about not being able to stop. The addiction had taken on a life of its own. I was powerless over cigarettes. I couldn't stop smoking.

It's hard to admit we are addicts. Who wants to think we are different from, or less than, other people who don't smoke or smokers who can stop with just one? We try to prove we're not addicted by attempting to control our addiction. For example, we limit ourselves to low-tar brands or limit where and how much we smoke. We play the powerful game of minimizing and denial as we get sicker and sicker in our addiction. Approaching late-stage addiction we may even withdraw from others when we smoke, trying to hide and keep secret our loss of control. Such was my progression, and apparently it is common. As a nicotine addict "hits bottom," he or she faces loss of control, depression, and hopelessness about smoking and the inability to stop.

Are we all equal in our addiction to cigarettes? Certainly not. Some of us seem genetically programmed for our drug of choice.[5]

Since smokers are not all alike, it's easier for some of us to stop drinking alcohol or coffee than it is to stop smoking. With other smokers, the opposite is true. The addiction to nicotine can vary widely.

Some researchers have described addiction as a two-step model, acquisition and maintenance.[6]

- The activity is new and pleasurable. It appears to satisfy our needs and provides a sense of well-being.
- The addict seeks to avoid the discomfort and unpleasant moods associated with withdrawal.

Other researchers have devised charts and written descriptions to divide the symptoms of alcoholism into three stages.[7] To get a clearer view of the progression of nicotine addiction it is helpful to adapt these basic ideas. There is always a danger in using charts or making statements of (inevitable) progression. Although these charts may be reliable for the earliest and most advanced stages, the intermediate stages vary greatly.[8] Charts of progression also give us a chance to strengthen our already powerful denial by telling ourselves: *I'm not that bad. All those things didn't happen to me.* Any chart is only a guide. Take what is useful and leave the rest.

Put check marks beside the items that apply to you so you can see how far your nicotine addiction has progressed. Remember that the written exercises in this book take time and that we nicotine addicts seem always to be in a rush. I gently support your *slowing down.* I encourage your *taking the time* for your recovery. You are worth it!

Exercise: How the Disease of Nicotine Addiction Progresses

Remember to *stop.*
Take three slow, deep breaths.[*]
Take your time as you complete the exercise.

Early-Stage Addiction
As I progress in my addiction, do I (or did I in the past)

____ smoke with friends?
____ smoke to calm my nerves?
____ want to keep smoking when others stop?
____ avoid places where I can't smoke?
____ often think about the next cigarette?
____ feel irritated when smoking is discussed?
____ minimize how much I smoke?
____ rationalize my smoking?
____ hide cigarettes so I won't run out?
____ crave the first cigarette in the morning?

Middle-Stage Addiction
As I progress in my addiction, do I

____ sneak cigarettes?
____ feel guilty each time I find myself smoking more cigarettes?
____ make frequent excuses for why I can't stop now?
____ feel unable to discuss my smoking?

---

[*]See page 4 for breathing instructions.

23

Your Story

____ try to prove to others and myself that I'm not addicted?

____ hear loved ones express concern about my smoking?

____ switch to low-tar cigarettes or limit the number I smoke?

____ have mood swings?

____ seem more at ease when I am smoking?

____ feel tense when I can't smoke?

____ increase my time alone so I can smoke?

____ keep breaking promises about stopping?

____ neglect eating to smoke?

____ have a decrease in sexual desire and ability to perform?

____ have sinus drainage and a cough?

____ make excuses about frequent illness?

____ experience nausea or loss of appetite?

____ have chest pain or poor circulation?

____ look forward to smoking alone?

____ feel a loss of energy?

____ blame stress for my smoking?

____ get headaches when I smoke?

____ attribute illness caused by smoking to other factors?

____ have smoking-related accidents—for example, burning myself or my possessions?

____ get short of breath with only moderate exertion?

____ start smoking binges when I am alone?

____ worry frequently about disease and death due to smoking?

____ have an acid stomach or peptic ulcer?

____ need medication to treat vascular disease, hyperacidity, or pulmonary disease, yet continue to smoke?

____ have infections and an increase in adverse drug reactions that cause more sickness?

____ have cancer?

Late-Stage Addiction

As I progress in my addiction, do I

____ find I cannot smoke as much as I used to?

____ seem to have exhausted all alibis?

____ feel totally unable to stop smoking?

24

____ see no possible solutions to help me stop smoking?

____ feel abandoned and hopeless?

____ feel burned-out physically, emotionally, spiritually?

Nicotine Is Addictive!

Many nicotine addicts who were addicted to cigarettes, as well as to other drugs, find it more difficult to stop smoking than to stop using heroin, alcohol, marijuana, cocaine, or prescription drugs.[9] Relapse is higher among smokers than among heroin users. Nicotine is six to eight times more addictive than alcohol. Nearly 77 percent of the nicotine addicts still smoking have tried, but failed, to quit.[10] In spite of knowing the health hazards and wanting to quit, 25 percent of the adults in our country continue to smoke.[11] This is mostly due to the addictive properties of the mood-altering drug, nicotine:[12]

- tolerance (more is required over time to achieve the same effect)
- withdrawal (symptoms develop when a person stops using the drug)
- drug-seeking behavior (behavior changes when the addict is deprived of a cigarette)[13]

Within the first few years the number of cigarettes a nicotine addict smokes gradually increases. A similar pattern of tolerance develops for heroin addicts.[14] Quitting on your own can be extremely difficult. The relapse rate for nicotine addiction, heroin addiction, and alcoholism is approximately 70 percent within the first three months.[15]

Former Surgeon General C. Everett Koop reported[16] that nicotine is as powerfully addicting as heroin and cocaine. His report also shows that nicotine addiction can be successfully treated.

Tobacco contains nicotine, a *stimulant* similar to cocaine and amphetamines. Also present is acetaldehyde, the first metabolic product of alcohol, which is much stronger than alcohol and has strong *sedative* properties.[17] No wonder tobacco can be used to wake us up and calm us down!

- Shallow puffs increase our alertness since low doses of nicotine cause the *release* of acetylcholine, a powerful stimulant.
- Deep drags relax us since high doses of nicotine *block* the flow of acetylcholine.

Who could ask for more in one drug? It's a stimulant for the weary and a tranquilizer for the anxious.

Nicotine seems to improve our ability to learn, pay attention, react, solve problems, and do still other tasks.[18] Many smokers believe that cigarettes reduce depression, stress, anxiety, and anger.[19] Smokers may interpret these as positive traits simply because they are receiving temporary relief from withdrawal symptoms as they continue to smoke.

Smokers are sensitive to the concentration of nicotine in the bloodstream. After a night's sleep, we inhale the first few cigarettes. This sends a burst of nicotine to the brain, producing an almost immediate sense of euphoria and satisfaction. Throughout the day, we manipulate the intake of nicotine by inhaling more or less. When too many cigarettes are smoked (of course, the number differs for each of us), acute toxic effects, resembling nicotine overdose, are felt: nausea, light-headedness, headache, weakness, and an increased heart rate.[20] When too few are smoked (usually less than ten), the nicotine level drops and we feel distress.[21]

Let's take the example of an eighteen-hour waking day for a two-pack-a-day smoker. This person spends three to four hours with cigarettes, inhaling one thousand milligrams of tar through four hundred puffs.[22] Say this smoker switches to low-tar cigarettes "for health reasons." This person will often increase the number of cigarettes smoked and will hold smoke in the lungs for longer periods of time, taking deeper puffs. Thus, the cigarette that is advertised as one to five milligrams of tar may actually be equivalent to fifteen to twenty milligrams of tar!

Even after I stopped smoking I missed the drug. I missed getting my fix. I did not miss the constant clearing of my throat, the cough, the headaches and nausea, the bad smell of my hair and clothes, the terrible taste in my mouth, the yellow stains on my teeth, the sneaking around for a cigarette—but I missed the drug of nicotine. I am grateful that today I don't miss that drug anymore, but I missed it often in early recovery.

The Damage

This is the information I wouldn't read about when I was smoking. What I thought then was, *I know cigarettes are bad for me but all those details are boring.* Actually, this was my denial and minimizing working overtime to keep me from the facts. Cigarettes kill and the details are important.

Cigarettes are known to cause more illness and death each year than *all other drugs combined.*[23] When we smoke, how much damage is really done? Approximately forty-eight million Americans smoke cigarettes.[24] Forty-five percent of smokers will die from a tobacco-caused disorder.[25] In 1992, we learned that smoking is responsible for 20 percent of all deaths in the United States. The 1989 Surgeon General's Report provided revealing information:[26]

- Nicotine is the leading cause of stroke, which is the third leading cause of death in the United States.
- Women's lung cancer rates have caught up with men's. From 1985 until the report was published, lung cancer and breast cancer tied as the leading cause of death in women.
- Forty-three chemicals in tobacco smoke have been proven to cause cancer.

If I were active in my addiction, I wouldn't read much more of this (assuming I had read this far). I didn't want to know. When I was researching this book, I was amazed at how little I actually knew about the health effects of smoking. Over the years, something in my brain would automatically switch off when I heard the details. I said to myself, I know smoking is bad for me but I don't want to hear anymore. *This was my attitude as I continued to zap my body for years after I knew that smoking was destroying me.*

Heart Disease

Smoking is a big factor in heart disease.[27] Coronary artery disease is three times more prevalent in smokers than nonsmokers between the ages of forty-five and fifty-four. As smokers, we have elevated levels of "bad" cholesterol (LDL), increased heart rate, and increased blood pressure. These contribute to arteriosclerotic disease in the coronary arteries, as well as in the peripheral vascular and cerebrovascular systems.[28] It's amazing that we don't *all* die early from heart attacks when we recognize what happens to our body. Specifically: As the total cholesterol is raised and "good" cholesterol (HDL) is lowered, blood platelets get stickier. This makes it more likely that a clot will form in our arteries that already have been narrowed by smoking. Combine this with a heart that is beating faster and requiring more oxygen at the same time that the carbon monoxide from smoking is reducing the amount of oxygen that the blood can carry.[29] It's a gruesome picture, but there is good news for those of us who stop smoking.

Your Story

Within one to two years after quitting smoking, our risk of dying from a heart attack is equal to that of someone who never smoked![30]

Cancer

For us smokers under the age of forty-five, lung cancer rates are eight times higher than for nonsmokers. Smoking is a major cause of cancer of the esophagus, larynx, and mouth. It contributes to cancer of the head, neck, bladder, kidneys, and pancreas.[31] But again, there is good news: Cancer risks decline after smoking stops. An ex-smoker, recovering for ten to fifteen years, has cancer rates comparable to someone who never smoked.[32]

Lung Disease

Smoking is the major cause of emphysema and chronic bronchitis, known as chronic obstructive lung disease, the fifth leading cause of death in the United States.[33] Smoking is responsible for the constriction of bronchial tubes and bursting of the *alveoli* (air sacs in our lungs). Carbon monoxide inhibits our ability to clear mucus from the respiratory tract.

As if that isn't enough, smoking causes much additional damage to our body's systems.

Reproductive system. Compared to women who don't smoke, we women who smoke have (a) babies who are more often born prematurely; (b) infants who can die more often shortly before or after birth (due to fetal tobacco syndrome); (c) have more spontaneous abortions;[34] and (d) may have earlier menopause. When we smoke and take birth control pills, we are more likely to have a stroke or premature heart attack.[35] We also have an increased risk of osteoporosis and cancer of the cervix.[36]

Respiratory system. Sudden Infant Death Syndrome and general respiratory distress of newborns is two times higher in offspring of mothers who smoke.[37]

Gastrointestinal system. As smokers, we are more likely to get peptic ulcer disease.[38]

Skin. Smoking reduces the elasticity of our skin, increases wrinkling, and makes us appear to be aging more rapidly.[39]

Smell. We smokers are twice as likely to have a reduction in our sense of smell.[40]

Bladder and urinary tract. We smokers have bladder tumors and urinary tract infections more often than nonsmokers.[41]

Nicotine reduces the effectiveness of many medications that are prescribed for illness. For example, medicine for peptic ulcers, blood pressure, and pain are often less effective for smokers.[42]

If you are still active in your addiction and have read this far, you might be thinking about taking a break and smoking a cigarette (if you are not already smoking). I can relate to that. I remember often smoking when I thought about the damage cigarettes were doing to my body. This may seem crazy to someone who doesn't smoke. The details of self-inflicted harm are painful and I, like other nicotine addicts, used cigarettes to medicate pain; so it was a vicious circle. I encourage you to not light up, but to tolerate the discomfort as you start to break the cycle of pain, medication, pain.

Passive Smoke

This is one of the saddest parts of all for me. For many years I smoked in the presence of my children and others I love. I forced them to become passive smokers. Addiction is a disease of denial, and my denial kept me polluting their air. Granted, for the last few years I smoked, I didn't smoke around nonsmokers, but by then I suspect I had already done a lot of damage to many clean pink lungs.

In 1972 the Report of the Surgeon General first raised the topic of "passive smoke," even though the dangers of smoking had been identified in that report every year since 1964.[43] In 1986 the Report of the Surgeon General included a section called "The Health Consequences of Involuntary Smoke." It asserted that "environmental tobacco smoke," now called *passive smoke,* is a serious health hazard and people should not have to breathe it.

What happens to us when we breathe passive smoke? The 1986 report reviewed data from sixty scientific studies and concluded that passive smoke causes cancer in otherwise healthy nonsmokers. A 1992 report confirmed that passive smoke kills thousands of nonsmokers each year, in addition to making children and other relatives very sick.[44] As they mature, the children of smoking parents may have more respiratory infections; often their lung function is less well developed. Physicians should now advise pregnant women to stay out of rooms where smoking is allowed because of the risk to the unborn child.[45] The evidence is clear: Smoke, ours or others', is dangerous to our health and to the health of those around us.

As women who smoke, we are more likely to have babies that weigh less than the babies of mothers who do not smoke.[46] Men who smoke are more likely to father babies who die or have serious health problems.[47] The effects mothers who smoke have on unborn children are well documented,[48] but studies of the effects of the father's smoking on the unborn child are new with less complete data.

Scientists at Yale University demonstrated that parents who smoke may increase the risk of their children developing lung cancer as the children grow up.[49] The study suggests that 17 percent of all lung cancer among people who never smoked may be blamed on early exposure to smoke in the home. Other research indicates that passive smoking may cause thirty-two thousand heart disease deaths every year.[50]

So should we switch to low-tar cigarettes? As far as passive smoke is concerned, the answer is no. A U.S. Department of Agriculture study shows that smokers who switch to low-tar cigarettes actually increase the health risk to themselves and others. Secondhand smoke from low-tar cigarettes has up to 30 percent more cancer-producing substances than smoke from high-tar cigarettes.[51]

Today I cannot tolerate spending much time in smoky environments. "Reformed smokers are the worst," they say and it may be true. I don't say anything aggressive to smokers; I just don't put myself in places where I have to smell someone else's smoke. When I am forced to be in smoky places, I get a sinus headache and I vividly remember how I felt most of my life.

I've done enough damage to my lungs, and I owe it to myself to not continue that damage. I have lived with nicotine and smoke since conception: I was usually in the presence of smoke, mine or someone else's, all of my life until four years ago. Today I say, No more.

The Ritual of Smoking

I went into a daze as I picked up my car keys and walked out the door. My resolve for "no more cigarettes" evaporated as I started the engine of my car. Again, I was in the ritual of driving to the convenience store to buy another pack. By the time I bought the pack and was back in my car, the craving that had started the ritual was gone. But, mindlessly, I opened the pack, removed a cigarette, put it in my mouth, and pushed in the car lighter. I inhaled deeply, and after the withdrawal symptoms subsided I thought to myself, Why did I do that? What is wrong with me?

A two-pack-a-day smoker feeds the addiction forty times a day, taking 140,000 drug hits a year. Many rituals are associated with the process. We carry the pack of cigarettes, open the pack, extract a cigarette, hold and light the cigarette, inhale and exhale the smoke, and put out the cigarette the same way thousands of times a year!

These little rituals give a sense of security to otherwise insecure lives. Life is change, but as nicotine addicts, we surround ourselves with the predictability of rituals that produce little trances as we space out and get our fix!

The fix comes fast, too. The effect of smoked nicotine is much faster than the effect of intravenous nicotine.[52] Ten seconds after inhaling, nicotine reaches the brain. The effect is almost immediate and the nicotine dose can be precisely controlled.[53] This is powerful reinforcement for the trance-inducing rituals associated with smoking. No wonder it's so hard to quit.

Quitting

For me, quitting was a process. I tried to stop smoking many times before I was successful. I felt like a failure each time I started smoking again. Today I know that all those times were practice in stopping and showed my willingness to keep trying. I learned much in my previous attempts, and the practice helps me stay stopped, one day at a time. Quitting was a process, not an event.

Most smokers wish they could quit.[54] Even though stopping smoking isn't easy, millions of Americans quit each year.[55] Recovery from nicotine addiction follows a general path, I believe, just as recovery from alcoholism follows a general path.[56] There are always exceptions and variations, but the trends are clear. Use the following exercise to learn where you are in the process.

It's important to take the time needed for your recovery. Even though you may feel rushed to get through this book, take your time. Your recovery is important and so are you.

Exercise: Recovery from Nicotine Addiction

Remember to *stop.*
Take three slow, deep breaths.
Take your time as you complete the exercise.

Your Story

Place a check mark beside the statements that are true of your current process. Remember we're seeking progress, not perfection.

As I progress in my recovery, do I

____ want honestly to stop smoking?
____ make an effort to learn about nicotine addiction?
____ go to therapy or a support group?
____ talk with other recovering nicotine addicts?
____ have a persistent desire to stay abstinent?
____ believe a new life is possible?
____ have a healthy diet and get adequate rest?
____ increase my exercise to a healthy, sustainable level?
____ feel an increase in energy?
____ feel better physically?
____ feel better emotionally?
____ show improved sexual performance?
____ have fewer mood swings?
____ apply new values of self-care to daily living?
____ have a growing desire to continue my recovery?
____ show changes that friends and family notice?
____ feel my self-esteem growing?
____ have a new circle of friends to offer me encouragement?
____ feel more emotional stability without cigarettes?
____ have a new appreciation of spiritual values?
____ feel greater peace of mind?
____ help others in their recovery?
____ feel content in my abstinence?

Withdrawal Symptoms

I was afraid of having withdrawal symptoms. I was afraid I'd lose control. My children asked if withdrawal would be so painful that I wouldn't be able to stand it—was that the reason I didn't stop? I did not know what to say. I had never gone for long without a cigarette nor experienced any real pain in the process. It was mainly the fear of losing control that seemed so scary when I anticipated facing withdrawal. When I stopped and experienced withdrawal, I was surprised.

It was definitely not the big deal I thought it would be. The physical withdrawal was mildly uncomfortable but not painful. Nor did it last long. I remember having a dull headache and feeling restless, but that was it. I got a lot of support from my friends and used the tools and strategies I am sharing with you in this book. It was not worth all the dread I suffered thinking about it.

About 80 percent of the smokers who stop smoking experience withdrawal symptoms: anxiety, restlessness, irritability, sleep problems, confusion, and impaired concentration.[57] Withdrawal symptoms begin within a few hours and peak in twenty-four to forty-eight hours. So the worst part of withdrawal is over in a couple of days. Some of the symptoms may appear up to four weeks after cessation, and hunger and cravings may last longer.[58]

What happens as we move from active addiction into recovery? What withdrawal symptoms can we expect when we stop smoking? Since most relapses happen within the first week[59] of smoking cessation, we need to know what the withdrawal symptoms are and how to handle them. This allows the symptoms to pass *without* picking up a cigarette to remedy them. We must stay vigilant about the power of the addiction: of smokers who stop, 75 percent return to smoking within three to six months.[60] The message is not to give up because of the odds. Rather, the odds indicate that this is not a simple job and that preparation is needed.

Emotional

Many of the early withdrawal symptoms are emotional; they relate to the new feelings we experience in early recovery. The next chapter talks about how to handle those feelings so that withdrawal can pass quickly and our recovery can progress uninterrupted by relapse.

Physical

The Cancer Information Service publishes a list of physical withdrawal symptoms that we will review in the next exercise.[61] They sharply decrease and are less severe after the first few days of smoking cessation, since most nicotine is gone from the body in two to three days.[62] During the second and third week the symptoms show even less severity. The reduction of symptoms is not consistent; there are ups and downs, but the withdrawal process does pass rather quickly. We will get better. Stopping and staying stopped keeps us from moving in and out of withdrawal.

Exercise: Withdrawal Symptoms

> Remember to *stop.*
> Take three slow, deep breaths.
> Take your time as you complete the exercise.

If you are in the process of withdrawal, take a separate sheet of paper and a pen or pencil and note after each symptom you are having how long it lasts, and what it feels like. I was surprised how short-lived the physical symptoms were for me. You may be, too.

Irritability. This lasts about two to four weeks and is often found in people who smoked heavily. Nicotine gum lessens the severity. Are you irritable these days?

Fatigue. After quitting, people who had smoked heavily suffer fatigue that lasts about two to four weeks. Nicotine gum lessens the severity. Are you feeling especially tired these days?

Insomnia. Frequent awakening is common for the first few days, as are dreams of smoking. The symptoms seldom last longer than one week. Are you sleeping as well as usual?

Coughing, nasal drip, and dry mouth and throat. These symptoms are the body's way of getting rid of mucus that previously blocked passages. The decrease in mucus production causes dry mouth and throat. The symptoms seldom last longer than a few days. Are you experiencing any of these irritations?

Dizziness. This is not a symptom of nicotine withdrawal. Dizziness is caused by more oxygen reaching your brain. Have you felt dizzy lately?

Lack of concentration. It takes the body two to three weeks to adjust to the lack of constant stimulation produced by nicotine. How is your concentration today?

Depression. Crying and depression may occur, but the feelings pass. Are you depressed?

Tightness in chest, headaches. Tension due to withdrawal passes after a few days. Chest muscles that are sore from coughing relax in a few days, too. Do you have chest pain or headaches?

Constipation, gas, and stomach pain. Nicotine withdrawal may cause a decrease in intestinal movement. The symptoms pass in a week or two. Is your digestive tract upset?

Hunger. Cigarette cravings are often confused with hunger. Nicotine gum helps lessen this symptom. The first week seems to generate the strongest cravings, which decrease in the next few weeks or months. Are you eating more than usual these days?

Craving for a cigarette. These are most frequent in the first few days. For most people, they decrease after two to three weeks. Intense cravings may come from time to time months or even years after smoking stops, but they pass quickly. Have you craved a cigarette lately?

Remember that the symptoms—all of them—are only temporary. It helps if we consider the symptoms a reminder of the powerful addiction we are facing. Instead of falling into the self-pity mode of "poor me" and "isn't withdrawal awful?" we can think of the symptoms we feel as "symptoms of recovery."

Pay Attention to Caffeine

Eighty-six percent of smokers drink coffee, a major source of caffeine.[63] (Other sources include chocolate, tea, and many soft drinks.) Smoking increases the metabolism of caffeine. When we stop smoking and don't change our caffeine intake, the caffeine levels in our blood increase by 50 to 60 percent. Then we may suffer increased anxiety and restlessness due to the effect of caffeine intoxication. It's easy to attribute this overdose of caffeine to nicotine withdrawal.[64]

On the other hand, if we stop using caffeine at the same time we stop smoking, we'll experience increased fatigue, headaches, and muscle twitches.[65]

How you handle your caffeine as you stop smoking is entirely up to you. I think it is a good idea to cut down on caffeine slowly during smoking cessation. You may find, as I did, that you feel very nervous and anxious when you use precessation levels of caffeine.

When we stop smoking, research shows that we actually decrease our anxiety.[66] I noticed this; you, probably will too. Anxiety reduction is a blessing. Don't let caffeine take away this wonderful benefit of not smoking!

How to Cope with Withdrawal Symptoms

When I had surgery years ago I expected a period of convalescence. I didn't plan a hectic schedule. I took it easy and I pampered myself. I did the same thing when I stopped smoking. I stayed away from smoking friends, I ate nourishing meals, I took long walks, I kept a leisurely pace for a few days. I was gentle with myself, and I spent time with others who were gentle with me, too. I drank herbal tea, I read short magazine articles (since my concentration wasn't up to par), and I kept phone numbers of caring friends with me at all times. I was amazed at how much time I had when I stopped smoking. I needed to fill that time with healthy and nurturing activities—not toxic smoke!

It helps to talk about your struggles with supportive recovering smokers and to know that the struggles will pass with time. Remind yourself that the symptoms are short-lived and that quitting, while difficult, is not impossible. If you do slip, don't be hard on yourself. Just get back on track as soon as possible. Here are some techniques to make the withdrawal process less difficult.[67]

Irritability. Use relaxation and meditation techniques, go for walks, take warm showers and baths (see also "Stress Management" on pages 95–97).

Fatigue. Take it easy. Nap when you feel the need. Don't expect too much from your body for a couple of weeks. Give it a chance to start to heal.

Insomnia. Use relaxation and meditation techniques[68] and abstain from caffeine after 6:00 P.M.

Coughing, nasal drip, and dry mouth and throat. For cough, sip warm herbal tea; for dry mouth, sip ice water or fruit juice; for dry throat, chew gum or suck cough drops or sugarless candies. The nasal drip as well as the other symptoms do not last long.

Dizziness. Be gentle with yourself. Take it easy. Remind yourself that dizziness is a sign you are getting more oxygen to your brain.

Lack of concentration. Again, take it easy. The concentration returns soon. Recognize that the most important thing is you not smoking today.

Depression. This effect often leads smokers to relapse. Be sure to read "Depression" on pages 78–80.

Tightness in chest, headaches. Use relaxation and meditation techniques; take warm showers and baths.[69]

Constipation, gas, and stomach pain. Drink six to eight glasses of water daily and add roughage (raw fruit, vegetables, whole-grain cereals) to your diet.

Hunger. Drink water and low-calorie liquids; eat low-fat, low-calorie snacks.

Craving for a cigarette. Use "The Serenity Prayer for Smokers" from Nicotine Anonymous (see the appendix titled "Nicotine Anonymous Materials"). This symptom often leads to relapse.

Benefits of Quitting

To my surprise, my cough disappeared almost immediately. I stopped constantly clearing my throat. My sinus headaches and nausea stopped, too. My toes tingled for a day or two as a larger supply of oxygen started to reach them. I awoke feeling refreshed, not hungover with a rotten taste in my mouth. Throughout the day, my mouth tasted fresh and the perfume on my body smelled fresh, not musty and smoky. I felt, looked, and smelled so much better! I was really happy not to be smoking.

The benefits of living a smoke-free life begin almost immediately. Remember that your body will start to heal itself within the first twelve hours after you quit smoking.[70] Here is a list of immediate benefits.

- Carbon monoxide in our blood declines within eight hours.
- Respiratory function improves; our cough and excess mucus production decrease rapidly.
- Smell and taste improve quickly.
- Oral health improves, as does our breath.
- Increased oxygen increases stamina and vigor shortly after quitting.
- Self-image is enhanced as abstinence becomes a reality.
- Twenty minutes after the last cigarette, the acute effects of increased blood pressure, pulse rate, and body temperature are eliminated.

Naturally there are several long-term benefits as well.

- Premature death risk is reduced. Within ten to fifteen years, as ex-smokers, our risk is comparable to someone who never smoked.
- After two to seven years, our risk of coronary heart disease equals that of a never-smoker. Our risk of heart attack starts to decline after only one year of abstinence!

- Our risk of lung cancer gradually declines, until ten to fifteen years after stopping we are no more likely than the never-smoker to get lung cancer.
- Larynx cancer rates decrease until, after ten years, they are equal to the risk of a never-smoker.
- Our risk of mouth cancer starts to decline in the first few years, approaching that of a never-smoker in ten years.
- Our risk of bladder cancer decreases in the first few years; after seven years of abstinence the rate approximates that of the never-smoker.
- Lung function improves for those of us who have not already sustained permanent lung damage.
- Our risk of smoking-induced stillborn babies and low-birthweight babies is eliminated if smoking stops by the fourth month of pregnancy.
- Peptic ulcers heal more rapidly in ex-smokers than in smokers.

Tips for Quitting

Support from other recovering nicotine addicts was crucial to me, especially early in recovery. I had attended several programs to stop smoking in the past, and I remembered some of the advice and tips I learned. I left the table as soon as I stopped eating and brushed my teeth. When I thought about cigarettes, I refocused my attention by saying, "I am grateful I don't smoke" and quickly changed my thoughts to a new idea. If I awoke in the morning thinking about cigarettes, I rinsed my mouth with diluted lemon juice to change the pH balance and the idea of cigarettes was quickly released. Brushing and flossing my teeth became frequent rituals throughout the day and evening. I stayed away from smoking friends for a while and avoided smoky places. I drank no coffee or alcohol. Instead, I drank plenty of water and walked several times a day, even if it was only for just a few minutes.

Catapres, a brand name for clonidine, has been helpful to smokers in reducing withdrawal symptoms, particularly cravings. It also appears that clonidine helps people to remain abstinent, particularly women. Behavioral counseling, however, is important and success is higher when clonidine is used with a stop-smoking program.[71]

Nicotine gum, which might be prescribed by a doctor, may also help us quit. The gum, however, needs to be used with some other form of stop-smoking program to be very effective. If we don't use behavioral counseling, our relapse rate is much higher. Also, we run a risk of long-term dependence on nicotine gum. For example, one study showed that 25 percent of the smokers who were treated with the gum were still using it one year after they stopped smoking.[72]

In addition to the gum, there are a variety of other nicotine replacement systems. Many smokers find that nicotine replacements help relieve withdrawal symptoms,[73] but they should be used in combination with a behavior change program.

The nicotine patch has been helpful to some smokers who want to quit; however, the patch provides a constant blood level of nicotine and does not deliver the "drug hits" that are so important to us. As you might expect, many addicts find the patches boring.

Like nicotine gum, the nicotine spray, and inhalers give us the drug hits we crave, but they don't deliver our nicotine with the same speed as smoking a cigarette. And, just like the gum, there may be a problem coming off the patch, spray, and inhaler without returning to smoking cigarettes. Remember, while these drugs are not magic potions, they can be helpful aids if used in combination with other recovery methods.

Smoking clinics, stop-smoking programs, and support groups are truly helpful. Many sources have compiled tips to help us achieve abstinence. Clinics and smoking cessation groups exist in nearly every community. Twelve Step programs (discussed in chapter 4), based on the Twelve Steps of Alcoholic Anonymous, are helpful to us. The telephone directory often lists "Smokers' Information" or "Smokers' Treatment" in *The Yellow Pages*. Most bookstores have several publications to help the smoker. The American Cancer Society, the American Lung Association, and the American Heart Association are all helpful resources.

Exercise: Tips for Kicking the Habit

Quitting smoking is a process, not an event. Everyone reading this book is at a different stage in the process. Remember this: You are exactly where you are supposed to be right now. You are further than you were yesterday, and tomorrow you will be further than today. With this in mind, try to find a creative and healthy reward for reaching this point. Next let's look at what positive steps you can take today to get yourself where you want to be.

- If you are at the point where you are currently smoking, and not yet ready to stop, try delaying that first cigarette of the day. If you normally smoke as soon as you wake up, wait until after your shower. This will give you some practice at not smoking. Keep a log of your use, and note stopping when you were able to delay smoking.
- If you are considering stopping sometime in the future, but don't have a specific stop date in mind, practice not smoking in just one situation. Delay smoking immediately after a meal. To do this, you need to plan an alternative activity. Try getting up from the table immediately and going for a short walk or doing the dishes. See how the urge for a cigarette will pass whether you smoke or not. This is a central lesson and one that will aid you as you progress in recovery.
- If you have set a stop date within the next month, you will need to make a plan for that day. Prepare your day in such a way as to avoid opportunities to smoke, and try to identify in advance places and people to avoid, as well as supportive people to be with. Practice in advance some ways to deal with stress without smoking, so that when the day comes, you will have some healthy coping skills to use.
- If you have quit today, or within the past six months, pay attention to how you deal with strong feelings and stressful situations. Make a journal of the things that work and the things that don't, and make a point to learn new skills from self-help books recovering friends, and trial and error. Remember that smoking was a tool that you used in the past that solved problems in the short term, but was ruining your health. You deserve to use tools that work and won't hurt you. You deserve to be a nonsmoker.
- If you have not smoked for more than six months, continue to expand your coping skills. You can never have too many healthy ways of dealing with life! Work on building your support network of people who share your basic beliefs about recovery, and avoid high-risk situations. Tests are for school, where the cost of not passing is not death!
- If you have had a lapse, learn what you can from the experience. It is not the end of recovery, but rather a necessary part of your recovery. Avoid negative self-talk, as it is never constructive, and we have all done enough of it in our active addiction. Allow yourself to be where you are today, and attend to your needs to reach your goal for tomorrow.

Above all, reward yourself for getting to this point in recovery. No matter where you are, you are exactly where you are supposed to be today!

Do I Have to Get Fat?

This was a big one for me—my fear of getting fat ran a close second to my fear of losing control in withdrawal. Neither happened. The first three months, however, I often thought about cigarettes and craved sweets. Instead of eating candy and drinking milk shakes like my craving directed, I drank orange juice and ate fruit. When I drank orange juice, the craving for sweets passed. I ate sensibly and exercised daily. After about three months, my body settled down and the cravings for sweets stopped. I had not developed poor eating habits in the meantime, so I did not get fat. I felt so happy about taking care of myself. I could not believe I was the same person. I was not smoking. I had not gone bonkers and obesity was not on the horizon. I simply felt good.

Decreasing my sugar intake helped reduce my cravings, both for food and cigarettes. The first three months, however, were difficult, but I was able to reduce the cravings and gain only eight pounds. I am grateful sugar and cigarettes are no longer big deals or obsessions in my life.

It appears that smoking affects weight. Many nicotine addicts believe that smoking keeps them from getting fat. They are often afraid to quit because they fear gaining weight; some smokers who have quit return to smoking as a way to control their weight.[74] Finally, some smokers, particularly women, will not even try to stop smoking because they are so afraid of gaining weight.[75] It's helpful to know that women appear to be less likely to gain weight if they use nicotine gum when they stop smoking.[76]

Although many smokers do gain weight after they stop smoking, weight gain is not inevitable. For those recovering smokers who do gain weight, the average long-term weight gain is only about five to ten pounds. Smokers who gain more than that are eating more. After nicotine addicts quit smoking, they usually increase their sugar intake. As ex-smokers increase their caloric intake, they gain weight.[77]

Smoking depresses appetite for certain foods. Rats given nicotine weigh less than rats not given nicotine.[78] When rats are taken off nicotine, they eat more sweets and weigh more. Female rats, taken off nicotine, eat more high-carbohydrate food and gain more weight than male rats.

Typically, smokers weigh less than nonsmokers. Research has shown that even though smokers weigh less, their body fat is distributed in a pattern that is associated with higher risk for cardiovascular problems.[79] So there is *no* medical justification to continue to smoke on the basis of possible weight gain.

Although these were experiments with rats and not people, researchers speculate that nicotine might reduce the insulin in our bloodstream.[80] Insulin is essential, especially for the metabolism of carbohydrates. Thus, lowered insulin may explain why smokers crave fewer sweets and store less fat than nonsmokers. People in withdrawal from alcohol, heroin, and tobacco addiction appear to crave sweets and carbohydrates.[81] If this is true, and it takes the body several months to adjust to new insulin levels, we can eat sugar substitutes and fruit as our body adjusts to new blood-sugar levels. (Pay attention to how these sugar substitutes affect you. Some substitutes, like sorbitol, seem to have a laxative effect.)

When smokers try to stop smoking and diet at the same time, they may be more likely to relapse with cigarettes. Increasing physical exercise when stopping smoking is much better than trying to stop smoking while dieting to lose weight.[82]

These strategies can help you to avoid compulsive overeating in early recovery. The following list gives general guidelines.

- Eat three meals a day.
- Make sure each meal has at least one form of protein (for example, meat, fish, eggs, cheese, peanut butter). The less fat consumed, the better.
- Limit your daily intake of milk to eight ounces of skim milk.
- Limit the starches you eat (crackers, cereal, potatoes) to no more than four servings per day.
- Avoid all cakes, pies, cookies, candies. If you don't avoid them, you will probably experience even stronger cravings for sugar. This is a cycle hard to break, so why start it?
- Eat canned fruit packed in its own juices or in water. Or, better yet, eat fresh fruit. Limit your intake of canned fruit to two servings per day.

A licensed dietitian or a physician who understands nutrition can help you develop a diet that is right for you.[83] It is worth the time and effort to learn healthy dietary habits in early recovery.

In the beginning of abstinence from nicotine, it is useful to alter the mealtime routine.

- Drink a glass of water before each meal.
- Take smaller portions and eat slowly in small bites.
- Put down the fork between bites.
- Take time to breathe deeply and relax as you pause between bites.
- Drink sips of water between bites.
- Skip dessert or eat fruit.
- Leave the table as soon as you finish eating. Brush and floss your teeth; wash the dishes, take a walk, or plan another activity.

When you are hungry and it's not time to eat, acknowledge that you are craving food but instead of eating, do something else. The hunger will pass. It will come and go, like the cravings for cigarettes. Realize you cannot change the fact that you crave food. But you can change what you *do* in response to that craving.

Nicotine alters the metabolism of smokers, so more calories are burned and fewer calories are converted to fat. We have known for some time that smokers burn more calories, at rest, than nonsmokers. Now we also know that smokers who engage in light activity burn more calories than nonsmokers.[84] It is very important to exercise when you stop smoking. Exercise increases the metabolism and helps with weight control. A brisk daily walk can be an important part of your physical self-care plan. It provides pleasant distraction and a chance to "stop and smell the roses" as a stress-reduction technique.

Relapse Warning Signs

My schedule was hectic and I often felt tired. Being tired put me at risk for a relapse since I had always used the drug nicotine to pep me up and keep me going. Instead of smoking, however, I learned to meditate to deal with my fatigue. Having intense feelings was another time I realized I was on shaky ground and more likely to think about smoking. When strong feelings surfaced, I learned to cope with them (using the methods I describe in this book) instead of smoking.

After we quit we must protect our recovery. We can learn to recognize conditions that may lead us to start smoking again. Relapse prevention specialists Terence Gorski and Merlene Miller suggest these common symptoms be dealt with promptly to protect our recovery.[85] A relapse does not happen the minute we pick up a cigarette. Relapse *starts* before a cigarette goes into our mouth.

Ripe for a relapse

Look for one or more of the following conditions:

- *HALT.* In Twelve Step programs, we're warned not to get too Hungry, Angry, Lonely, or Tired. It's a good reminder to avoid relapse.
- *Expecting perfection from ourselves and others.* Learning to live and let live is a challenge.
- *Impatience and frustration.* Patience not only with ourselves but also with others is difficult for a nicotine addict. It's hard to accept that things will not always go as we wish.
- *Cockiness.* Believing we have everything under control can be a set up to light up. Be careful of this one.
- *Dishonesty.* These little lies come from people-pleasing, from not wanting to hurt or disappoint others, and from rationalizing and being dishonest with ourselves.
- *Thinking negatively and forgetting gratitude.* When we have a negative outlook or take things for granted, we can fall into self-pity and that may lead us right back to cigarettes.
- *Self-pity.* Wondering why things happen to us, becoming overwhelmed, and believing no one appreciates us are dangerous to a nicotine addict's abstinence from cigarettes.
- *Use of mood-altering chemicals.* It's hard to stop smoking if we drink alcohol or take medication or other drugs that alter mood. It's easy to lose our abstinence from cigarettes when we are under the influence of other chemicals.
- *Depression.* If we become depressed we need to talk with someone about it and treat it effectively.
- *Exhaustion.* As nicotine addicts, we are prone to ignore our internal cues that tell us we need rest. We must begin to listen to our body's needs.

Physical, emotional, and spiritual self-care are the answers to help us avoid the pitfalls that precede picking up that first cigarette after a period of abstinence. Take the time to develop these programs. As you do, you begin to accumulate insurance against pitfalls that may threaten your recovery.

Physical Self-Care in Recovery

As I progressed in my recovery from nicotine addiction, physical self-care became very important to me. When I was smoking, my body was simply something that carried my head around. My body needed to look good enough not to embarrass me. Beyond those two functions, my body was not something I valued. Today I care about my body and have a program for self-care that is an important part of my life.

Exercise: Checklist for Physical Self-Care

Remember to *stop.*
Take three slow, deep breaths.
Take your time as you complete the exercise.

The following checklist gives the crucial aspects of a self-care plan that I recommend to clients and follow myself. Use it to help you decide what goals you want to establish. You have read this book so far: Now it's time to ask, *What am I willing to do for myself in my physical recovery?*

_____ Maintain adequate nutrition with three meals daily and snacks (as needed).

_____ Sleep six to eight hours each night.

_____ Exercise fifteen to twenty minutes a day, three times a week.

_____ Follow a daily personal care routine.

_____ Abstain from alcohol and other drugs.

_____ Use a minimum of sugar and caffeine.

_____ Receive weekly therapeutic massages.

_____ Find a balance between work and leisure.

_____ Get regular physical and dental checkups.

SUMMARY
- Nicotine is a powerful, mood-altering, addictive drug.
- The longer we smoke, the greater the damage.
- Physical damage from smoking cigarettes can be devastating!
- The withdrawal symptoms, though unpleasant, pass rather quickly.
- The physical benefits of abstinence are substantial and begin soon after we stop smoking.
- There are many tips for quitting; resources and support groups are available.
- The journey we are embarking on is hopeful and exciting! All of our efforts now are practice in stopping for good.
- We live our life one day at a time, and that's the way we quit smoking.
- Weight gain can occur in early recovery, but there are effective ways to keep our weight within the desired range.
- A plan of physical self-care is essential and the benefits of putting one into action can be great!

CHAPTER 3

Emotional Recovery

NICOTINE SUPPRESSES FEELINGS. During withdrawal and early recovery, feelings often emerge with frightening intensity. This
intensity can lead us to relapse. We need to learn a better way
than lighting a cigarette to cope with our feelings. Exercises like
the ones in this chapter help us manage our strong feelings so
we can achieve long-term abstinence from cigarettes!

Feelings are very important. We experience and express emotions through our skin, muscles, and many other parts of our
body.[1] Feelings tell us about our basic needs and provide energy
that intensifies our life.[2]

We have spent most of our nicotine-addicted life learning to
control and cover our feelings with defenses. We may have been
raised in a family where there were spoken or unspoken rules
about expressing feelings. Here is a list of some messages we may
have received.

- Don't be unhappy. You have no reason to be unhappy.
- Don't cry. You shouldn't be upset.
- Don't cry or I'll give you something to cry about.
- Boys who cry are sissies.
- Girls are only pretty when they smile.
- Don't be angry. You have no reason to be mad.
- If you can't say something nice, don't say anything at all.
- Don't upset your mother or father.

When we suppress feelings with nicotine, we may become
depressed, get physically sick, and medicate with other addictions. Actually, the entire area of emotional health is starting
to be reevaluated and called into question.[3] Often symptoms
of addiction, codependency, and the results of a painful childhood have been mistaken for mental illness. What a relief it is to
learn we are not crazy! If our tendency is to smoke every time we

have a strong feeling, then learning to handle feelings is very important for nicotine addicts, as we'll see in this chapter.

Nicotine addicts often use cigarettes as our main way of coping with stress. Stress can be healthy or unhealthy, depending on how we handle it. When we medicate ourselves with nicotine to cope with stress, the stress just accumulates. We smoke instead of relaxing, behaving assertively, or managing our time properly. Since stressful situations often lead us back to our addiction, we need to learn and practice strategies to cope with stress so we don't have to light up.

Some researchers believe that people in recovery from addiction must deal with issues around codependence.[4] They believe it's important to increase our awareness of internal events (feelings and needs) and decrease our focus on how others see and evaluate us. I believe if these issues are dealt with, we can reduce the probability of lighting up again.

Core Issues: An Introduction

Dr. Charles Whitfield describes core issues that need to be addressed before emotional healing can occur.[5] They include grieving, "being real" (being who we really are in contrast to presenting ourselves as we think others wish to see us), neglecting our own needs, being overly responsible for others, low self-esteem, control and all-or-nothing thinking, and trust. Other core issues include identifying and expressing feelings, high tolerance for inappropriate behavior, fear of abandonment, difficulty handling and resolving conflict, and difficulty giving and receiving love. Based on my clinical experience, I believe these issues underlie recovery from all addictions, and I strongly recommend recovering nicotine addicts become familiar with Dr. Whitfield's approach.

Other authors have also written about core issues in recovery from codependency.[6] I have included the core issues I found most relevant in my process of healing emotionally from nicotine addiction.

- *Compulsive behaviors.* Identify compulsive behaviors that limit your emotional growth and develop a program of recovery to deal with them.
- *Defenses.* Learn what your defenses are, how they protected you in your addiction, and decide how to use them today.

- *Feelings.* Learn how to identify, accept, and express feelings of anger, shame, fear, sadness, loneliness, and happiness. Work through grief. Learn to be assertive. Address depression and anxiety.
- *Self-concept.* Recognize the influence of learned sex roles, family roles, definitions of success and perfectionism; learn how to handle compliments and criticism.
- *All-or-nothing thinking and control.* Moderate your all-or-nothing thinking and develop strategies to deal with control issues.
- *Boundaries and trust.* Recognize all-or-nothing trust issues and learn how to set healthy personal boundaries as you build trust in yourself and in others.
- *Inability to play.* Learn the characteristics of healthy fun; learn how to play and relax.
- *Stress management.* Identify the parts of your life where you feel stress and learn to meet your needs in healthier ways; choose stress-reduction techniques that are safe and healthy.
- *Intimacy.* Learn how to enhance intimacy and rebuild emotional connections that were lost in nicotine addiction.
- *Emotional self-care.* Develop guidelines for your self-care program.

In each core area you will find checklists, questionnaires, and a variety of exercises to help with your recovery. I encourage you to take the time to thoughtfully consider and complete them.

Layers

It helps to see the first three core issues (compulsive behaviors, defenses, and feelings) as layers in a circle.

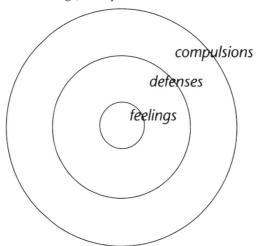

When we peel off one layer we reveal another. For example, when we strip away our compulsive behaviors we reveal our defenses; when we cast off our defenses we reveal our feelings.

Compulsive behaviors limit our emotional recovery. If we cannot move beneath that layer, we cannot progress. Nicotine addiction and other compulsions form a thick shell that keeps us out of touch with the sensitive feelings inside.

Psychological defenses are right underneath the compulsions. They maintain the compulsions and keep us from feeling the vulnerable emotions inside. When we peel back these defenses, we can challenge our compulsions and release our feelings.

Feelings are at our very center. Here is the private world that may be closed to others—or even to ourselves. In recovery from nicotine addiction, it is important to get to know ourselves. We must learn to deal with our feelings or when they surface, we will probably light up again.

Once we stop smoking and move through the layer of defense, the feelings we find at our center are special, *all* of them, even the sadness, loneliness, fear, and anger. All these feelings are important. In recovery we will come to value our feelings instead of gassing them with smoke.

These are the same feelings you had as a child, before you started to shut them off. If you're like most smokers you grew up too fast, took on roles that didn't allow you to express your feelings and, eventually, found nicotine as an effective drug to stop the feelings.

Surprise! Those feelings are *still* there. They've been safely stored under the layers. They are the precious, vulnerable part of you. This is the part that has been called the "inner child," the "child within," and the "magical child."[7] It is your emotional center. It has been alive since you were born, even though you have been out of touch with it for a long time.

Feelings are the wonderful, yet challenging, part of us that surface spontaneously when we stop smoking. As we recover, more and more of them become available. Life becomes fuller and more beautiful. When we bring our emotional center into more conscious awareness, we move not only to our own inner core but also open a door to become closer to others.

All of our feelings, even the anger, tell us how we need to lead our lives. We start to feel grateful for the storms as well as the rainbows. Our feelings give meaning and power to our lives as we stop drugging and gassing ourselves.

To claim emotional wholeness we need to accept and value ourselves for having our feelings (all of them); recognize the difference between having a feeling and acting on it; and learn what to do instead of lighting up.

The other core areas of recovery covered in this chapter keep us from knowing ourselves, too. If we know ourselves we'll be less likely to be caught off guard and turn to our old behavior, smoking, to cope.

Exercises and Their Benefit to You

I ask you to take some risks in this chapter, to do some exercises that may seem silly at first. But my clients do them and so do I. They are valuable. I encourage you to work through your embarrassment and self-consciousness.

One of the things I ask you to do in some exercises is to write about your feelings with your nondominant hand. For instance, if you typically write with your right hand, now write with your left hand. When you write with your nondominant hand, the writing may look like that of a child, and you tend to use more spontaneous words. My clients use this technique with much success, as do I and other therapists.[8]

Another exercise I ask you to do is to draw with crayons or colored pencils. Like using your nondominant hand, this may seem silly and you may feel embarrassed. It's OK to feel that way. They're just feelings. Acknowledge them and then, if you are willing, complete the exercise.

This book has limited space, so you will need additional paper on which to do the exercises. This requires more preparation time and energy for you: someone who is probably in a rush. I encourage you to slow down and take the time you need. I think you'll be surprised and pleased if you give the exercises a fair trial.

Why are these exercises helpful? Perhaps they encourage us to use a different area of the brain than we normally do. Perhaps they prevent us from defending ourselves with our usual sophisticated verbal skills. But learning why these strategies work is less important than giving them a try.

The rest of the exercises use questions and checklists that I have adapted from addiction and codependency literature or have developed with clients to help them work through the core issues they face. Nicotine addicts, as mentioned, are often in a hurry. I encourage you to slow down and answer each question in writing. Your emotional healing is worth the extra time this takes.

You will see that each core issue closes with several affirmations. There are many effective ways to use these short, simple, gentle, and positive statements. Say them silently or aloud. Write them down on paper or have someone read them to you. Tape them and play the tape back to yourself. Affirmations are an important part of healing.[9] They can help start new patterns, help you to start talking to yourself positively. Again, this takes time but it's worth it. Shortcuts in recovery don't pay. Remember that smoking cigarettes took a lot of time, too.

Core Issue One: Compulsive Behaviors

Cigarette smoking is the compulsive behavior we have in common, or you wouldn't be reading this book. It is one of the most insidious mechanisms, ever, for keeping us from knowing who we are, how we feel, and what we need.

Imagine what life would be like without this cycle of smoking:[10]

- *Preoccupation.* Why do I smoke? How do I stop? Can I keep smoking? Where are the cigarettes? Where is my lighter?
- *Ritualization.* Mindlessly picking up a cigarette, putting it in my mouth, lighting it.
- *Compulsivity.* Smoking whether I want to or not.
- *Despair.* Shame and guilt for continuing to smoke, leading back to *preoccupation* again: Why do I smoke? Why can't I stop?

Other major indicators that we are caught in this cycle are sneaking and lying about our behavior, denial, blaming, mood swings, isolating to engage in the behavior, physical symptoms, and loss of personal values.[11]

We nicotine addicts are compulsive people.[12] So we may have compulsive behaviors, other than smoking, that slow us down in our recovery. Using a separate sheet of paper, begin now to evaluate your compulsive behaviors.

Exercise: Compulsive Behaviors

Remember to *stop.*
Take three slow, deep breaths.
Take your time as you complete the exercise.

Charles L. Whitfield defines eight compulsive behaviors:[13]

Codependence. "Suffering and dysfunction associated with or due to focusing on the needs or behaviors of others."

Chemical dependence. "Recurring trouble associated with drinking or using other drugs."

Compulsive gambling. "Recurring trouble associated with betting, gambling, investing or financially risking in any way."

Workaholism. "Working to the detriment of our relationship with ourself or with others, especially family or other close people."

Sexual addiction. "Sexual activity of any kind, including repeated fantasizing, that recurringly interferes with or substitutes for our relationship with oneself or with others, including our spouse."

Rage-aholism. "Recurring use of fits of anger or rage to control, manipulate, or avoid authentic relationship with self or others."

Religious addiction. "A recurring pattern of using religion in any one or a combination of ways: judgmentalism, righteousness, rigidity, or as a way to alter one's state of consciousness, usually used unconsciously, to avoid our authentic relationship with oneself, others and our higher power."

Eating disorder. "A recurring pattern of any one or a combination of: overeating, bingeing, purging, not eating or overeating alternating with dieting or compulsive exercise, usually used unconsciously to avoid authentic relationship with self or others."

Research shows that if smokers are to be successful, they cannot ignore other compulsive behaviors. Take alcohol for example, 15 to 20 percent of heavy smokers have current alcohol problems. Unless these smokers stop drinking, it is unlikely they will be successful in smoking cessation.[14] Abstinent smokers who continue to drink alcohol are more likely to return to smoking.[15] Many smokers who are recovering alcoholics and drug addicts worry that if they stop smoking, they will relapse with alcohol and drugs. This seldom happens. Eighty to 85 percent of the recovering alcoholics in recent research reported no increased cravings for alcohol when they stopped smoking. Nor did they relapse with alcohol when they stopped smoking. As a matter of fact, stopping smoking may actually help recovering alcoholics and drug addicts not relapse with alcohol and drugs![16] Further, research indicates that treatment of smoking may be effective during or after treatment of alcoholism.[17]

There is definitely a major connection among nicotine, alcohol, and other drugs. Smokers who actively engage in other compulsive behaviors may also have a lower success rate in stopping smoking or be more likely to relapse if these behaviors are not acknowledged and addressed.

Your Story

Make a few notes beside the compulsive behaviors with which you can identify: Indicate (1) when the behavior was a problem for you and (2) how your life is being affected by that problem today. *You may also appreciate the insight that comes from noting anyone in your family who might have had one of these compulsive behaviors.* If you have a family history of substance abuse and other compulsive behaviors, you may be at a much higher risk for that problem yourself.[18] Addiction is a family disease; and it is interesting and useful to make connections between then and now.

Here are some activities that could also be compulsive and make our life unmanageable. We may use some of them as a way to cope with feelings. The activities provide a sense of pleasure or escape that actually affect us chemically,[19] as well as psychologically. Put a check mark by any of the activities that you may respond to compulsively.

_____ shop	_____ shoplift
_____ clean	_____ pull my hair
_____ take dangerous risks	_____ lie or exaggerate the truth
_____ watch TV, videos, sports	_____ exercise

Use these questions to help define which activities may be a problem. First, read the question and then insert the activity(ies) that apply for you.

- Do I_____when things are not going my way?
- Do I want to_____when I am bored?
- If I've been scared or angry, do I find myself thinking I should _____?
- When I feel "all alone," do I want to_____?

Here are several helpful hints to deal with compulsive behavior.

- Abstain from the behavior, one day at a time. Don't project going through the rest of your life without it.
- When the idea of this behavior comes into mind, ask yourself, *What am I trying not to feel?*
- Join a Twelve Step group and work with other people who share a similar problem and who are working a program of abstinence and recovery. See pages 118–119 for a list of Twelve Step programs.
- Continue your recovery by learning how to identify your feelings and needs—scheduling some therapy sessions may help in this process.

Affirmations are also helpful in dealing with compulsive behavior.

- I deserve a life free of compulsion.
- I can allow my feelings to come and go without having to push them down by_____(list the compulsive behavior here).
- I am powerless over my obsessions and compulsive behaviors, and I cannot do it alone. I can ask for help.

Core Issue Two: Defenses

Several psychological defenses protect your disease of addiction and encourage you to keep smoking. These are the defenses that may come up in your recovery and encourage you to pick up a cigarette.

Exercise: Defenses

Remember to *stop.*
Take three slow, deep breaths.
Take your time as you complete the exercise.
Put a check mark by the defenses that you use as excuses to keep smoking.

____ *Denial.* Other people are addicted, not I. I can stop anytime I want.

____ *Minimizing.* It's not that bad. I have only one vice.

____ *Rationalizing.* I'm going to die sometime, anyway. If it's not from smoking, it'll be from something else.

____ *Entitlement.* I've done a good job, or I've worked all day, etc. I'm entitled to a cigarette as a reward.

____ *Blame.* If I didn't have to put up with him or her or it, I could stop. Now is a bad time to stop because of him or her or whatever.

____ *Self-pity.* I am so overwhelmed with things right now, and it's so hard to stop smoking. I don't know if I'll ever be able to stop. I just can't do it. I'm too weak a person.

For smokers, self-pity is a major obstacle to stopping and staying stopped. When we stop smoking we need to feel our feelings freely and let them pass. Instead we say: (1) I don't want to deal with all this right now; (2) I don't want to stop, there is too much going on;

(3) It's too much for me; (4) I'm too old to stop; (5) I've already smoked too long.

We are often embarrassed to have strong feelings. We may believe it is self-indulgent to face and focus on our feelings. But it is *more* self-indulgent to avoid feelings and complain about the pain we would have if we stopped smoking. We nicotine addicts use discomfort as an excuse to return to smoking.

Smokers hate to feel uncomfortable, so we indulge ourselves in a drug to keep from feeling. What we really need is to have the courage and honesty to face our feelings, experience them, and let them pass.[20]

How do you protect yourself from pain? Previously, you smoked and the drug numbed you. When you put down your cigarettes, you may find that other defenses rise to the surface to keep you from feeling your feelings. Put a check mark by the defenses you use to avoid your feelings.

_____ I change the subject.

_____ I pace

_____ I blink back tears

_____ I swallow nervously.

_____ I hold my breath.

_____ I intellectualize, explain, or try to understand.

_____ I chatter.

_____ I eat.

_____ I give advice when not asked.

_____ I try to control the situation.

_____ I chew gum.

_____ I use humor (make fun of myself, use sarcasm or jokes).

We can use these and many other defenses. Often, when we have a strong feeling we use one of our defenses and our feeling seems to disappear. Thinking about problems abstractly (worrying) can keep us from dealing with our emotions.[21] When we find ourselves worrying or doing one of the things on the list, we can stop and ask, *What am I trying not to feel?*

Most of us are not aware of the extent to which we use defenses to keep our feelings from rising to the surface. By avoiding our feelings, we cut off the most valuable feedback we have about who we are and what we need. It takes time and practice to identify the defenses that keep the feelings inside. The best way to handle defenses is to be aware that they exist, pay attention to how we use them, and choose when we want to use them.

Using affirmations in your daily life may help. Here is a list of affirmations that can help deal with defenses.

- As I learn more about myself, my defenses become less automatic.
- I can slowly let go of the masks and defenses I used to use.
- I don't have to close myself from feelings by using my defenses.
- I don't have to keep pretending I am someone else.
- Learning to trust myself, and safe people, is better than any protection from defenses, but it takes time and I am learning to be patient.

Core Issue Three: Feelings

One of nicotine's prime effects is to suppress feelings and keep them from becoming too intense.[22] In recovery we are often scared that their intensity will overwhelm us. We forget that feelings come and go in a matter of seconds. We forget that feelings are not actions. We forget that, although we are powerless over our feelings, we can choose how we *act out* our feelings. Many of us never learned how to identify and express them in a healthy way.[23]

Feelings are strong cues to light up.[24] They can cause us to relapse. Our nicotine recovery is precious, and we must learn to handle feelings without smoking.

Let's begin by taking a closer look at the feelings of anger, shame, fear, sadness, loneliness, and happiness. In this section of the book, we will complete an exercise on working through grief and learning how to be assertive. We will also pay attention to anxiety and depression, which can cause problems for us in nicotine recovery.

First, let's look at how feelings were expressed in our families.

As children, we had feelings and we watched others to see if they did, too. We learned how to express our feelings by watching our families and friends express their feelings. This early learning continues to affect us today, and it's important to have insight into that effect. Take a look at what you learned in your family.

Exercise: Feelings

Remember to *stop.*
Take three slow, deep breaths.
Take your time as you complete the exercise.

How were these six feelings expressed by these people (you, your

family, and others) when you were a child? For example, what did
your father say and do when he felt these feelings? What did your
sister or brother do when she or he felt these feelings? Take time to
write what you remember on a separate sheet of paper.

Person/feeling	Anger	Shame	Fear	Sadness	Loneliness	Happiness
Father						
Mother						
Sister						
Brother						
Others						
Self						

Did your family encourage healthy expression of all these feelings?
Who was *allowed* to express feelings? Which feelings were not expressed by anyone? Did family members smoke or drink instead of
expressing feelings? Did people work all the time so they were emotionally unavailable?

As a child, you had the entire range of feelings, but if the feeling
wasn't expressed by others, you probably learned to numb yourself
when that feeling arose in you. Now, in recovery, the job is to undo
that numbing.

If you took the time to complete this exercise, you now have some
insight into why it was difficult for you as a child to express a wide
range of feelings in a healthy way. That learning affects you today.
It's no one's fault. The purpose is not blame but insight.

What do these significant people in your life say and do today
when they have these feelings? Does anyone smoke, drink, or work

"all the time" to keep from feeling emotions? Please make notes on a separate sheet of paper. Take your time.

Person/feeling	Anger	Shame	Fear	Sadness	Loneliness	Happiness
Father						
Mother						
Sister						
Brother						
Others						
Self						

Please answer the following questions about your emotional recovery on a separate sheet of paper.

- Do you continue to suppress feelings the same way family members did when you were a child?
- Do you and those you love display a wide range of feelings or only a few?
- What are you willing to *do* as part of your emotional recovery, now that you have new insight about feelings?

This chapter gives many examples of how to identify and express a wide range of feelings. What are your goals for expressing feelings? Make a few notes on a separate sheet of paper.

Automatically, we keep old patterns alive.
History repeats itself. We re-create our past.
The first step in changing is to see the pattern.
With self-awareness, we begin to have choices
and break the cycle.

Your Story

Anger

Let's gain more insight into how we learned to deal with our anger. Some of these exercises may seem silly and embarrassing at first. Please try them anyway. By giving ourselves time to overcome the initial resistance, we can benefit as we get in touch with our feelings.

Exercise: Anger

Remember to *stop.*
Take three slow, deep breaths.
Take your time as you complete the exercise.

Close your eyes and take a few deep breaths. Picture yourself as a child. Give yourself time to get a picture in your mind. Your age doesn't matter. Just get a picture.

All children feel angry sometimes. Did you express your anger? If you did, what happened to you as a result? Close your eyes again and remember a time that you, as a child, felt angry. Now open your eyes and use your nondominant hand to write on a separate sheet of paper about what happened. Be sure to keep writing until your story is complete.

Try to remember how you felt as a child when a parent became angry. Close your eyes and find a memory. Then open your eyes and write about that memory with your nondominant hand.

How do you feel today when someone around you expresses anger? Close your eyes and remember a recent time. Now open your eyes and write about these feelings with your nondominant hand.

Are you afraid people will leave you if you show your anger? (Even simply saying you are angry is showing your anger.)

Are you afraid of losing control if you feel your anger? (Remember that *feeling* angry and *acting* on it are separate things.)

People who get headaches, stomachaches, backaches, or feel tired or depressed are often people who keep their anger inside. Do you have any of these physical symptoms? Are you a person who keeps anger inside?

The next time you start to have one of these symptoms, stop and ask yourself, *What am I trying not to feel?* Write the answer with your nondominant hand.

It may seem foolish to you, a mature adult, to draw a picture to express a feeling. But again, I ask that you take a risk and try it. Take a separate sheet of paper and draw a picture of what your anger looks like. Use crayons or colored pencils. Take your time.

> Automatically, we keep old patterns alive.
> History repeats itself. We re-create our past.
> The first step in changing is to see the pattern.
> With self-awareness, we begin to have choices
> And break the cycle.

There are healthy and unhealthy ways to express anger. The unhealthy ways are destructive and unacceptable in healthy relationships. Perhaps you experienced them in your family. See if you can identify any patterns. A list of unhealthy ways follows.

- Rage-aholism is the "recurring use of fits of anger to control, manipulate, or avoid authentic relationships with self and others."[25]
- Verbal abuse uses criticism, shame, and demeaning language to belittle the listener: it is experienced as painful and humiliating.
- "Battering people with logic and arguments" is done to dominate, to leave the listener feeling trapped and "talked at."[26]
- Physical abuse is the use of violence, usually to control or harm another.

What angry response do you want to change? Do you scream, yell, throw things, swear, eat food, drink alcohol, get busy, or just *light up?* Following is a list of healthy ways to express anger.

- Make a "problem list" to define what you need to change: for example, your expectations, the situation, your response.
- List the advantages and disadvantages of your response to anger. Look at the feelings beneath the anger. Were you ashamed, embarrassed, self-conscious, afraid, sad, lonely?
- List alternatives to practice instead of your usual anger response. Ask for help if alternatives don't come to you naturally. Two healthy responses are to talk about being angry and to talk about the feelings beneath the anger. There are always feelings beneath the anger. If you can identify and resolve them, you will be in much better emotional shape.

- If your anger tells you that you are being violated, ask an impartial third party to help you sort through your options. Otherwise you continue to be a victim, awaiting the abuser's miraculous personality transformation (which seldom happens). If you have been emotionally, physically, or sexually abused, see a therapist to help you work through these issues.
- Collect information and keep an anger diary. Review your diary every few weeks to see if you are making progress. If you don't see changes and feel stuck, see a therapist.
- Develop assertive methods to express your anger, while avoiding blaming, sarcasm, name-calling, and physical attack.[27] Assertiveness books and classes are useful. Therapy, too, can be a helpful option.

Affirmations about anger are essential in recovery from nicotine addiction. When we stop smoking, strong anger often surfaces. Pick a few affirmations. Write them down and keep them with you. Practice them when you feel angry. *Use them.* If you don't get into new habits, you may start smoking again instead of coping more effectively with your anger.

- Anger doesn't have to run my life any more. I can express it safely and turn to others for help and support.
- I can make rational and healthy decisions about how to express my anger. I can admit my anger. I don't have to get headaches, backaches, and stomachaches, or suffer from depression because I am keeping my anger inside.
- Anger is just a feeling. It comes and goes like all my other feelings.
- Others won't abandon me if I say I am angry. I don't have to act violently or abusively; I can merely say that I am angry.
- Being angry doesn't mean anyone has to get hurt.
- When I am honest about my anger I can clear the air.

Shame
Shame says we are flawed and deficient.[28] It is different from guilt, which tells us we feel bad about something we have done, tells us we *made* a mistake. Shame tells us we *are* a mistake.[29] Shame is a universal human emotion. One of the reasons we feel shame is that we cannot live up to the perfection and ideal we hold in our limitless imagination.[30] Many smokers, particularly those of us who are perfectionists, experience shame when we stop medicating our feelings with nicotine.

To be close and intimate with other people, we must begin by feeling vulnerable and exposed.[31] This often brings up feelings of shame. There can be no intimacy unless we expose the most vulnerable parts of our lives to others, but this can be very painful.

Since shame has such far-reaching effects, let's look at it more closely. How does shame develop? What are its effects?

I felt so much shame when I smoked. I wanted to stop but could not. I promised to quit and broke my promises. I was a poor role model for my children, and with my secondary smoke, I injured their health and the health of other loved ones.

Exercise: Shame

Remember to *stop*.
Take three slow, deep breaths.
Take your time as you complete the exercise.

List on a separate sheet of paper several areas in which smoking increased your shame.
Do you ever feel self-conscious, not just when you're smoking but at other times, too? Do you say, "I feel nervous" or "I feel anxious," when you actually mean you feel self-conscious?

When are you likely to feel self-conscious (at a party, in a group of strangers, when standing in line, when someone is watching you)? List those places on a separate sheet of paper.

When you feel self-conscious, try saying: *I feel self-conscious*. Just keep saying that to yourself until the feeling passes. The paradox is that when you admit your feeling, it is likely to pass much more quickly. Try it.

If we grew up in certain perfectionist family structures, we are more likely to have developed shame. Here is a list of family rules that promote shame.[32]

- Always do the right thing.
- If it doesn't go as planned, blame yourself or someone else.
- Always be in control.
- If you're in control, do whatever it takes to stay there.
- Stay out of touch with your feelings.
- Be a human "do-ing," not a human "being."

What rules did your family have that helped to promote your feelings of shame?

At this point you may or may not identify with "shame"; however, you can probably recognize some of its physical characteristics.

- making no eye contact and hanging the head down
- feeling frozen and unable to speak
- feeling confused due to racing thoughts
- having an urgency to hide
- having a profound sense of being alone
- feeling a sense of transparency (others can see through you)
- apologizing to others for needs, feelings, and even just being[33]

Exercise: Dealing with Shame
Have you ever experienced these symptoms of shame? Make a few notes on a separate sheet of paper about the events and your response.

If we were shamed for our feelings as children, we can expect certain things to happen as we stop smoking and our feelings become more obvious to us.[34] To feel anything strongly may bring a sense of panic. We sense danger and react by pushing down our feelings. We may also react by going numb inside and by withdrawing from those around us. Were you shamed for having and expressing feelings? Does that early learning interfere today?

If we have been shamed for our needs in childhood, then, when we stop smoking and our needs become more apparent to us (since we are no longer anesthetized) we will likely feel ashamed and disgusted for having needs.[35] It may be difficult to express our needs to others because we feel yucky about having them. Take time now to write how you feel about being needy.

One way many smokers cope with shame is to try to look good and to try to manage everyone's impression of us. This produces self-consciousness. Can you relate to this? If so, write down how.

Another way we cope with shame is to run a self-critical script in our minds much of the time. Do you do this? If so, write down what this script looks like.

Automatically, we keep old patterns alive.
History repeats itself. We re-create our past.
The first step in changing is to see the pattern.
With self-awareness, we begin to have choices
and break the cycle.

Using a separate sheet of paper and crayons or colored pencils, draw a picture of your shame.

As we read and learn more about the effects of shame, we recognize that we are not unique in our pain.[36] We learn strategies to help us walk through the shame so that we may reveal, to safe people, who we are and thus develop the intimacy that was impossible in our active addiction to nicotine. We can begin to heal our shame when we stop smoking.

- Develop a support system of safe people to whom you can tell your secrets and receive validation for being a good person.
- Establish a spiritual program of recovery to connect with your Higher Power and goodness from within. Meditate and use visualization techniques.
- Use affirmations and daily readings to promote self-acceptance.
- Address your compulsive behaviors and destructive relationships—they feed the shame and keep strong the cycle of secrets.

Affirmations that help us to deal with shame speak of us as sacred human beings who are worthy of recovery. Choose several affirmations that you need to hear and repeat them several times a day.

- I am glad I was born.
- I deserve a place on this planet.
- I am worthy of love and recovery.
- I am a special human being.
- I am a creative and spirit-filled person.
- My feelings and my needs are very important.

Fear

Many fears are normal in recovery from addiction.[37] We fear withdrawal symptoms and the physical and emotional pain that may surface when nicotine is removed. We fear being with people without the medication of our cigarettes. We fear we will look bad, show our anger, and so forth.

Your Story

When we stop smoking we feel all our feelings more intensely—fear is no exception. We may even fear the intensity of *all* our feelings. Recognizing that many ex-smokers relapse when intense feelings surface, we should be prepared to deal with this fear.

Talking about our feelings is the first important step. This is difficult when dealing with fear since many of us believe that saying we are afraid shows that we are not strong. We'll look at our reactions to fear in the following exercise.

Exercise: Fear

Remember to *stop.*
Take three slow, deep breaths.
Take your time as you complete the exercise.

Close your eyes and picture yourself as a child. Remember a time when you were afraid. When you have a memory, open your eyes. Write about that memory on a separate sheet of paper using your nondominant hand.

When you were afraid as a child, how were you treated? Were you ignored, punished, ridiculed, or told not to be afraid? Were you listened to and comforted? Write down how you were treated.

As a child, before you started smoking, how did you learn to cope with being afraid? Write down ways you were taught to cope.

After you started smoking, how did you cope with feeling afraid? Did you light up and worry? Did you light up and pour a drink? Write down ways you coped.

Close your eyes and recall a recent time when you were afraid. When you have the memory, open your eyes and use your nondominant hand to write about what happened. Did you share your feelings with others? Did you ask for help? How did it feel to be afraid if you were alone?

Now complete this sentence: Today, when my loved ones are afraid, this is what I do and say:

Automatically, we keep old patterns alive.
History repeats itself. We re-create our past.

The first step in changing is to see the pattern.
With self-awareness, we begin to have choices
And break the cycle.

Now, on a separate sheet of paper, draw a picture (with crayons or colored pencils) of how your fear looks.

The next time you are afraid, just say to yourself, *I feel afraid*. Repeat it to yourself until the feeling passes. Instead of telling yourself *not* to feel afraid, accept that *it is OK to be afraid*. Again, the paradox: When you embrace your feeling, it goes away. And guess what? It goes away *without* having to gas yourself with smoke.

Affirmations can help you when you are learning to face your fear. Choose the ones that fit and repeat them when you feel scared (but are not in *physical* danger).

- It's OK to feel scared. It's just a feeling and it passes.
- Feeling scared doesn't mean something bad is going to happen.
- When I am afraid I can remember the closeness of my Higher Power.
- I can feel scared and still have the courage to act.
- When I face my fear and walk through it, peace follows.
- Peace awaits me when I place my fear in the hands of my Higher Power and know that I am all I need to be.
- I can release nagging fears and know that all is well.
- I have the courage to make life-enhancing decisions.

Sadness

Feelings of sadness tend to emerge as we stop smoking. We can feel sad even after the withdrawal symptoms pass. It's helpful to gain insight about how we experience and express sadness. Answering the questions in the following exercise will provide some insight.

Exercise: Sadness

Remember to *stop.*
Take three slow, deep breaths.
Take your time as you complete the exercise.

Close your eyes for a moment and remember a time when you were sad as a child. When you have the memory, open your eyes. Use your nondominant hand and write about it. Were you allowed to cry? Did someone comfort you? Take your time and remember your sadness.

When you were growing up, how did you feel when someone else in your family was sad? Did you think it was your job to cheer them up? Were you afraid when someone felt sad? Did you feel angry? Close your eyes for a moment and find a memory. Then open your eyes and write about your memory with your nondominant hand.

When you are sad today, what do you say and do?

When you smoked, how did nicotine affect your feelings of sadness? When you'd light up, did the feelings go away?

How do you feel today when other people are sad and what do you do? Is it hard not to smoke when other people are experiencing intense feeling?

> Automatically, we keep old patterns alive.
> History repeats itself. We re-create our past.
> The first step in changing is to see the pattern.
> With self-awareness, we begin to have choices
> and break the cycle.

Now, using a separate sheet of paper, draw a picture (with crayons or colored pencils) of how your sadness looks.

When you feel sad, say to yourself, *I feel sad. It's OK to feel sad.* Continue saying this until the feeling passes. If tears come, that's fine. Crying is a good way to release sadness. Tears are very healing. Expressing your sadness through tears is a healthy way to handle sadness. Smoking is not.

If you feel embarrassed about crying, say to yourself, *I feel embarrassed about crying.* Continue saying this until the embarrassment passes; then say to yourself, *I feel sad and it's OK to feel sad.* Keep saying this to yourself, or to a safe friend, until the feeling passes. (*Safe people* are those who listen to what you say *without* giving advice, criticism, or judgment, or telling you "you shouldn't feel that way." Trust your feelings about who is safe.)

Learning to deal with your feelings will take practice. Be gentle and patient with yourself. It took years and thousands of puffs of smoke to learn to effectively suppress your feelings. It will take time to learn that feelings are just feelings; they come and go quickly if you just acknowledge them.

Sadness is an important feeling and deserves affirmations. Choose a couple of the following affirmations and practice them when you feel sad.

- Accepting my sadness heals my pain and helps it pass.
- Sadness softens me to others and helps me be more sensitive to their pain.
- Sadness means loss, and I need to let go of the old to make room for the new.
- Feeling my sadness is healing and brings personal growth.
- Sadness comes and goes quickly. Self-pity can last a lifetime. I will embrace my sadness and release it without clinging to self-pity.
- Joy and sadness are natural rhythms, like the ebb and flow of the tides.

Loneliness

Addiction is a disease of isolation and nicotine addicts, even if we appear outgoing, are often intensely lonely people. When we give up our cigarettes we give up the most important relationship in our life. We feel abandoned: lost and alone. We must deal with loneliness without picking up a cigarette.

Loneliness in recovery may be a problem for several reasons.[38] Genuine intimacy may be blocked by unresolved grief or by our underlying sense of inadequacy (shame), which may keep us isolated and unable to share secrets or fears. We may be so afraid of feeling lonely and abandoned that we cling to emotionally dead relationships. Perhaps we cope by being so busy that we have little time to develop mutually nurturing relationships.

Feelings of loneliness can be strong cues to relapse with nicotine, and we must be prepared to deal with them.

Exercise: Loneliness

> Remember to *stop*.
> Take three slow, deep breaths.
> Take your time as you complete the exercise.

When you were lonely as a child, how were you treated? Were you ignored, punished, ridiculed, and told not to be lonely? Did anyone listen to you and comfort you? Using a separate sheet of paper, write down your memories.

When your parents were lonely, what did they say and do? Remember to include their compulsive behaviors (for example, smoking, drinking) if applicable.

When you smoked, how did you handle your loneliness (put a check mark by the categories that fit):

____ Went to a party and smoked, giving yourself the illusion of being close to other people.

____ Poured a drink, felt sorry for yourself.

Smoked as you got busy to forget your loneliness.

Automatically, we keep old patterns alive.
History repeats itself. We re-create our past.
The first step in changing is to see the pattern.
With self-awareness, we begin to have choices
and break the cycle.

On a separate sheet of paper, draw a picture of your loneliness.

Using your nondominant hand, write about what it was like for you to be lonely as a child.

When you are lonely, admit it to yourself and tell someone else. Find someone to tell who won't deny your feelings (by telling you not to be lonely, giving you advice on how to be less lonely, etc.). Simply acknowledging your loneliness is the first step in dealing with it. If you feel embarrassed when you start to admit private, vulnerable emotions, say to yourself, *It's OK to be embarrassed about sharing my feelings. I've done everything possible to keep them a secret for a long time.*

The more often we acknowledge the feeling, the less of a big deal it is. Recovery is about having fewer big deals. We need to be patient with ourselves because nicotine took care of the big deals for many years. Recovery is a process, not an event.

Here are affirmations I find helpful. Try them when you feel lonely.

• I can be alone without being lonely. I can savor the solitude that connects me with my inner wisdom.

• I can be with affectionate, caring people and leave the prison

of loneliness and isolation.
• I will never leave me. I will always be with me.

You have now completed exercises for five different feelings: anger, shame, fear, sadness, and loneliness. You are developing insight about these feelings, and it's helpful to share that insight with safe people from your support system.

You may also want to share your drawings. When you've found safe people and shared, make notes on a separate sheet of paper about your experience of sharing.

Happiness

I was driving on a street in Harrisburg about a year after my last cigarette. It was a beautiful day. I was thoroughly enjoying my life at that moment and I felt very happy. Then, the thought occurred to me: *Now it's time for a cigarette*. At that moment I realized that any intense feeling could trigger the idea of lighting up, even a pleasant feeling like happiness!

Happiness is a feeling, like all other feelings and can trigger thoughts and cravings for a cigarette. So let's learn how to handled feeling happy, and wanting to celebrate, without smoking a cigarette.

Exercise: Happiness

Remember to *stop.*
Take three slow, deep breaths.
Take your time as you complete the exercise.

When you were a child, did you feel happy in your family? When you felt happy, were you afraid the reason for your happiness would be taken from you? Some children feel bad about being happy when a loved one is in pain. Other children think that happiness is one of the few feelings allowed because it denies pain and shows that "everything is fine," even when it isn't.

What was it like in your family? Close your eyes and take a few deep breaths. As you do, picture yourself as a child. When did you feel happy? Was it OK to show your happiness? Were you expected to act happy, even if you were not? Take your time to let the memories, thoughts, and feelings come to you.

After you open your eyes, use your nondominant hand to write what you remember on a piece of paper. You may want to talk about this with a safe friend.

Your Story

Some of these affirmations may be helpful to you:

- It is OK for me to feel happy.
- I can be happy and celebrate without poisoning my inner child.
- Happiness is a gift we are granted. Feeling happy is a byproduct of other life experiences.
- Happiness comes and goes like all other feelings.
- I can welcome happiness as a gift I deserve.
- Happiness is not "out there." It lies within me. I can encourage it to spring forth.
- I don't need to be wildly enthusiastic or deadly serious. I can focus on the middle ground and have fun and cultivate a sense of humor.
- Happiness is a feeling like all other feelings. It does not have to overwhelm me or push me to act on impulse. Long-term happiness is not the product of short-term gratification.

Grief

When we lose something important, such as nicotine, we have a "grief reaction." The next exercise helps us learn more about grief so that we can help ourselves through this part of our emotional recovery.

Exercise: Grief

> Remember to *stop.*
> Take three slow, deep breaths.
> Take your time as you complete the exercise.

When ending the cycle of nicotine addiction, you suffer a real loss. Put check marks by the signs of grief you are experiencing at this point in your recovery.

Preoccupations
____ My life could have been different if I hadn't smoked.
____ I think about disease or death due to smoking.
____ My obsession with cigarettes will never go away.
____ I have other thoughts (list them on a separate sheet of paper).

Confused thinking
____ What do I do next?
____ How do I act without smoking cigarettes?

____ Why do I feel confused?

Feelings
____ I feel alienated.
____ I feel sad.
____ I feel afraid.
____ I have uncontrollable emotions.

Spiritual crisis
____ I feel an emptiness or void.

In what stage of grief are you now?[39]

____ Denial and isolation
____ Anger with self, others, God
____ Bargaining and denial: *Maybe I'm not really addicted. Maybe I can smoke just one.*
____ Sadness over losses, "wasted" parts of life, etc.
____ Letting go and acceptance

To assist in the grieving process, certain steps are crucial. Check which areas you are now addressing:

____ I am building a support system that will nurture me through the grieving process and encourage and validate me as I deal with my loss of nicotine.
____ I am working a Twelve Step program to deal with denial and with other recovery issues of powerlessness, personal short-comings, amends, and forgiveness.
____ I am developing my spirituality through prayer, meditation, creativity, and so on, to fill the void left by the loss of the addictive cycle.

Following are recommendations for dealing with grief. Use the ones that you think will work for you.

• Don't replace your loss with food or another addiction. Give yourself time to grieve.
• Let your feelings come and go. Don't try to stop the pain; be with it.
• Talk to safe people about the pain. Don't avoid or change the subject if it surfaces. Identify it and share it.

- Take all the time you need. It's important not to hurry.

Affirmations can help you in the grieving process. Practice the ones that speak to your grief.

- Loss is painful, and I must allow myself the time to cry and grieve.
- It's important to feel my feelings as I say good-bye and let go.
- Tears cleanse my soul and free me to move on.
- Freedom is the other side of grief. I deserve to move through the grief to freedom.

When grieving the loss of nicotine, you may begin to remember *other* losses. Examples of loss include the following: part of yourself (through illness, injury, body image, profession, lifestyle); an important person or relationship (through death, abortion, divorce, abandonment, geographic move); possessions (money, home, objects).

If you experienced a loss and did not deal with it at the time, you probably have some unresolved feelings. You may need to feel them before you can let go in a healthy way.

Acknowledge the feelings and talk about the losses with other recovering people. The feelings are just feelings. They will pass, whether you smoke over them or not.

Exercise: Stages of Grieving

Remember to *stop.*
Take three slow, deep breaths.
Take your time as you complete the exercise.

Complete the following section by listing three of your significant losses. List the loss you experienced, your age at the time, the way you coped with your loss at that time (were you smoking or active in another addiction?), and your current stage of grief (where are you now in moving through the stages of grieving?).

The stages of grieving include denial, isolation; anger with self, others, God; bargaining ("if only"); sadness over loss; letting go; acceptance.

If sadness, loneliness, or anger starts to surface as you are completing the exercise, be sure to call someone in your support system instead of lighting a cigarette. Exercises like this one prove, more than ever, that nicotine is a powerful drug to medicate feelings; we crave it when strong feelings start to surface.

Loss/Age	Coping strategy	Current stage of grief
	Smoking? ___ yes ___ no Other addictions:	____Denial, isolation ____Anger with self, others, God ____Bargaining ("if only") ____Sadness over loss ____Letting go, acceptance
	Smoking? ___ yes ___ no Other addictions:	____Denial, isolation ____Anger with self, others, God ____Bargaining ("if only") ____Sadness over loss ____Letting go, acceptance
	Smoking? ___ yes ___ no Other addictions:	____Denial, isolation ____Anger with self, others, God ____Bargaining ("if only") ____Sadness over loss ____Letting go, acceptance

Don't smoke over the feelings, just *acknowledge* them. Acknowledge that it is OK to have strong feelings; *label them* (sad, angry, scared, lonely) and *share them* with someone else. Then, using a separate sheet of paper, write about them with your nondominant hand.

Next, draw a picture of the feelings you had when you wrote about your losses. Take however long you need, and the feelings will pass without smoking another cigarette.

Remember that all our feelings are important. They should be identified and shared with safe people. This is crucial to emotional recovery from nicotine addiction! Many nicotine addicts relapse because strong feelings emerge and they pick up a cigarette instead of repeating an affirmation and otherwise dealing with the feelings. Because this is so important, I want to stop here and offer some more affirmations about feelings. Please take the time to read them slowly and repeat them often. It's difficult to communicate how *very* important this is to your recovery.

- Feelings are a natural part of me. I can accept them uncritically and appreciate the depth they add to my life.
- I can face my feelings and experience them fully. They are just feelings and they will pass.
- All my feelings are very important. I no longer need to hide them behind a smoke screen.
- I will pay attention to my feelings and their location in my body. (Use the ones that apply to you: A tight throat or a tense neck or a stomachache may mean you are angry. A heavy chest may mean you are sad. Nausea may mean you feel ashamed.) I don't have to get sick; I can just talk about my feelings.
- My feelings are worthy of attention. I need to talk about them so I don't act them out.
- My feelings are temporary and pass quickly if I just acknowledge them.
- My feelings are an expression of my uniqueness. No one has the same emotional life I do.

Assertiveness

Smoking anesthetizes us—we don't know when we are being taken advantage of or pushed around. When the smoke clears and our feelings start to emerge, anger tells us what was hidden: For example, we now see that our boundaries are not being respected by others. We must take action. It's difficult to say no, but it is a necessary part of setting healthy boundaries for ourselves.[40]

No doubt this feels scary to smokers who have spent years trying to avoid conflict. Guess what? Conflict doesn't have to be painful, and we can learn to be assertive without being aggressive. Assertive people communicate openly and honestly about their feelings and needs.

Instead of lighting up when our boundaries have been crossed, we can behave assertively. Smokers need a lot of work in this area, and there's no time like the present to get started.

Exercise: Assertiveness

Remember to *stop.*
Take three slow, deep breaths.
Take your time as you complete the exercise.

Let's look at the ways we typically express feelings, needs, and ideas.

What style is yours?

In the passive style, I
____ avoid expressing my feelings so no one gets upset.
____ avoid asking for what I need, for fear I may impose on others.
____ avoid expressing my ideas so no one is offended.

In the aggressive style, I
____ try to persuade others to feel the way I do.
____ tell others what I need and coerce them into giving it to me.
____ try to convince others to agree with my ideas, continuing until they agree or there's a blowup.

In the assertive style, I
____ express my feelings, recognizing others may feel differently.
____ express my needs, recognizing that if they can't be met one way, they can be met another way.
____ express my ideas, recognizing others need not agree with me.

Here are some typical responses, according to the three styles. What do you say?

Passive style
____ I feel the same way you do (whether this is true or not).
____ I'll meet your needs (no matter what price I have to pay).
____ I agree with your idea (no matter how much integrity I lose).

Aggressive style
____ You have to feel the same way I do. I'll convince you.
____ If you don't meet my needs, you'll pay a price.
____ If you don't agree with me, it's because you don't understand.

Assertive style
____ This is my feeling. It's OK if you don't agree.
____ This is what I need. It's OK if you don't meet it; I have other resources.
____ This is my idea. It's OK if you don't agree.

This is a small sample of the many choices we have. Which pattern is dominant for you? In recovery from nicotine addiction, we know what our unmedicated feelings, needs, and thoughts are. We have choices about how we wish to express ourselves. We can express ourselves with honesty, dignity, and self-respect.

Most nicotine addicts need training in assertiveness. Excellent resources are available.[41]

Use the following affirmations to help you become more assertive.

- I have the right to be assertive.
- I have the right to say no.
- I have the right to be myself.
- I have the right to my own thoughts, feelings, and identity.
- I take action to change self-defeating behavior.
- I deserve to be personally powerful.

Address Depression and Anxiety

Depression

When we stop smoking we may wonder about the difference between normal feelings and feelings caused by withdrawal and grieving our loss of cigarettes. There is no one easy answer, but the exercises we've completed so far can help us begin to understand part of the picture. As time passes, withdrawal subsides and grief passes; the picture gets clearer.

We may also wonder about the difference between normal feelings and feelings we have when depressed. The feelings most often associated with depression are fear, anger, and sadness, so we'll focus on them.

Fear can be healthy if it protects us from a danger or from acting on impulse. When we are depressed, fear often feels like a hole in the pit of our stomach. We may refuse to be left alone or we may isolate ourselves from others. Normal fear comes and goes rather rapidly but, in depression, dread and doom hang over us. With normal fear, we may feel brief, limited tension. When we are depressed we may be restless and have bouts of panic. As we anticipate the worst we may get sweaty palms and other symptoms of intense anxiety.

Anger can be a great protection. It can tell us that something is wrong and that we need to take action, such as saying no, or changing our expectations of ourselves or others. When we are depressed we may not be aware we are angry, but we'll have physical complaints: headaches, stomachaches, backaches, allergies. Sometimes, in depression, anger comes out as rage, sarcasm, blaming, striking out and wanting to hurt another person.

When we are not depressed we may experience similar reactions to our anger, but they will be shorter and we will not obsess about them.

When we are depressed, the sadness hangs over us for a long time; normal sadness, by contrast, comes and goes rather quickly. In depression we have a very negative opinion of ourselves: We are self-critical; we negatively interpret most of the events around us and anticipate a bleak future; we exaggerate, overgeneralize the negative, and ignore the positive.[42]

When we are depressed we often have sleep problems. It's hard to concentrate and memory problems are common. These symptoms are also found in early withdrawal from nicotine, but they are transient and should pass within a few weeks. If these symptoms continue, it's good to contact your doctor.

When depressed, we feel overwhelmed and may believe we cannot go on. If this feeling lasts long or if suicidal thoughts occur, contact your doctor. Today, depression is treatable with antidepressants that are not addictive and have fewer side effects than remedies from years past. I recommend that you also receive psychotherapy if you take antidepressants, since drugs alone are seldom the answer.

It is important to treat depression. Some people notice an increase in depression after they stop smoking.[43] This may be particularly true for women.[44] The lesson here is not to keep smoking. Instead, treat the depression if it appears or worsens during or after smoking cessation.

Antidepressants might be useful for smokers who have trouble quitting.[45] Thirty to 40 percent of smokers have a history of depression, and it may help to treat their depression before smoking cessation begins.[46] Recent research indicates an antidepressant called bupropion (the generic name for Zyban) has shown effectiveness in reducing cravings.[47] When we are depressed we may not be effective in our efforts to stop smoking. Becoming depressed after stopping smoking may result in a relapse unless the depression is successfully treated.[48]

Please contact your doctor if you are currently taking medication for depression or anxiety and have just started to not smoke, one day at a time. Nicotine affects some medications by making them stronger or weaker.[49] Ask your doctor if you need to increase or decrease your medication as you continue your abstinence.

Your Story

In the past, we may have medicated our depression by smoking. When we stop smoking, the depression may become more obvious. It's important to remember that treatments are available that show positive results. It makes sense to avail ourselves of the latest developments, both in the fields of medicine and psychotherapy. I strongly support you treating your depression—if it is a problem—and not return to smoking. Cigarettes never helped anyone.

Here are some affirmations that will help you deal with depression.

- One day at a time.
- This, too, will pass.
- It's good to pamper, not pity, myself.
- I can take one constructive action today.
- I don't have to do it alone. I can ask for help.

Anxiety

When I was smoking, I believed nicotine calmed my anxiety. I often felt like I was about to jump out of my skin. I thought smoking helped me cope with my anxiety. I was afraid I'd lose control and "go over the edge" without cigarettes. Actually, it worked in the opposite direction. When I was smoking, I experienced the reduction of nicotine withdrawal symptoms every time I'd light up. What addict doesn't "feel better" after a hit?

As I abstained from cigarettes, reduced my caffeine and increased self-care, I experienced more internal peace and comfort than I can ever remember feeling before. What a blessing!

Exercise: Anxiety

Remember to *stop.*
Take three slow, deep breaths.
Take your time as you complete the exercise.

Anxiety has physical, emotional symptoms that can result in barriers to nicotine recovery and spiritual growth. What are your signs of anxiety? Place a check on the symptoms for experience.

Physical signs of anxiety
____ Shakiness
____ Chest pain

____ Rapid heartbeat
____ Burning stomach
____ Headaches
____ Difficulty breathing
____ Dizziness or lightheadedness
____ Muscle aches and pains

Emotional signs of anxiety
____ Irritability
____ Edginess
____ Excessive worry
____ Sleep problems
____ Tension
____ Fatigue
____ Poor concentration
____ Fear of losing control

If you are still smoking and thinking about stopping, or if you have started abstaining, one cigarette at a time, you may be feeling anxious now. This is normal. Physical withdrawal symptoms can lead to a temporary increase of anxiety. These symptoms do not last long if you take care of yourself and get the help and support you need.

Any change, even positive ones, can produce fear and an increase in anxiety. Addicts hate to be uncomfortable so, typically, we do whatever we can to avoid changes (even when the changes are good for us).

In recovery, we learn that there is a difference between acting-out impulsively and making constructive changes in our lives. We make choices that are good for us. We learn to "feel the fear and do it anyway," while getting the help and support we need.

Research shows that when we abstain from nicotine, our anxiety level has a chance to decrease. Within a couple of weeks, if not sooner, you will probably begin to experience less anxiety.[50] This is exactly what happened to me, but it's the opposite of what I expected!

Of course, we can help ourselves by doing the footwork of adequate self-care. Too much sugar and caffeine can increase anxiety. Meditation and prayer are helpful in reducing anxiety. Exercise is good, too. Marathon running is not required; a simple walk can make a difference.

We don't have to do anything perfect; this pressure just creates more anxiety. As addicts, we are prone to extremes. Let's just be gentle with ourselves and practice being mindful of the importance of self-care and balance in our lives.

If an increase in self-care and support do not reduce your anxiety, it may be helpful for you to consult your physician. Ask your doctor to "rule-out" physical causes for your anxiety. If there are not physical malfunctions contributing to your anxiety, your doctor may recommend medication.

Many antidepressants help reduce anxiety, so I prefer that my clients take those medications and stay away from the addictive anti-anxiety drugs. (The last thing an addict needs in recovery is a prescription for addictive drugs!) Please discuss this with your doctor.

It may be helpful to work with a therapist, too, as you learn to identify and express your feelings in a healthy, smoke-free way and work through your codependency issues. Also, I encourage you to look for people in recovery who "have what you want" in dealing with stress and anxiety without smoking.

Core Issue Four: Self-Concept

We learn roles from the time we are small children.* For nicotine addicts, these roles become our identity. Our self-concept is largely based on them. We learn what it's like to be "successful" as a woman or a man from what we observed in our family.

Chances are you played more than one role in your family. You may still be playing one of these roles. Nicotine addicts live behind a smoke screen, operating on automatic pilot. Becoming aware of your role helps you choose whether you want to modify it. See if you can identify which role you played in your family.[51]

The *hero* strives to perform well and make the family proud. The hero seeks to be approved, successful, and helpful. Working to the point of exhaustion to "look good" becomes a frantic way of life. The hero's major strength is being a hard worker and an

---

*All roles originally published in *The Family Trap,* 1976 © by Sharon Wegscheider-Cruse. Also published in *Choicemaking,* 1986 © by Sharon Wegscheider-Cruse, Health Communications.

effective organizer. Inside, however, the hero generally feels guilt and inadequacy. Here is what the hero needs to learn.

- It's OK to be a human being instead of a human "do-ing."
- It's OK to make mistakes. We don't have to be perfect.
- It's OK to ask for help. We don't have to do everything alone.
- It's OK to be vulnerable and show feelings.
- It's OK to stop "fixing" other people and pay attention to our own needs.

Exercise: Hero
If you are acting the role of a hero today, what do *you* need to learn? Please write your answer on a separate sheet of paper.

The *scapegoat* acts out and becomes the problem child, defying and challenging authority and probably abusing chemicals. The scapegoat seems to create trouble wherever he or she goes. Although the scapegoat has major assets such as good insight about reality, sensitivity, and creativity, inside the scapegoat is very lonely and is hurt at not being heard. Here is what the scapegoat needs to learn.

- It's OK to show the hurt that's underneath the rage.
- It's OK to stop rebelling and to start negotiating.
- It's OK to say no without being hostile.
- It's OK to ask for and receive emotional support.
- It's OK to tolerate feelings without medicating with drugs.

Exercise: Scapegoat
If you are a scapegoat today, what do *you* need to learn? Again, write your answer on a separate sheet of paper.

The *lost child* is withdrawn and solitary, usually alone in his or her room: reading, drawing, listening to music. Often we don't even miss the lost child! Patience, creativity, and independence are the lost child's strengths; inside, however, the lost child feels loneliness and rage. Here is what the lost child needs to learn.

- It's OK to reach out to others, even though it's hard because we're shy.
- It's OK to face pain instead of losing ourselves in books, music, art, hobbies.

Your Story

- It's OK to show others who we are.
- It's OK to form close relationships.
- It's OK to be seen.

Exercise: Lost Child

If you are a lost child today, what do *you* need to learn? Please write your answer on a separate sheet of paper.

The *mascot* is the center of attention, funny, cute, and, perhaps, hyperactive and clumsy. This person takes the pressure off social gatherings since people focus on the mascot's antics. The mascot's strengths include humor and knowing how to enjoy him- or herself. Inside, however, the mascot fears falling apart and not belonging. Here is what the mascot needs to learn.

- It's OK to assume responsibility.
- It's OK to let others entertain themselves.
- It's OK to risk being serious.
- It's OK to be assertive.
- It's OK to have safe people touch us.

Exercise: Mascot

If you are a mascot today, write what *you* need to learn on a separate sheet of paper.

> Automatically, we keep old patterns alive.
> History repeats itself. We re-create our past.
> The first step in changing is to see the pattern.
> With self-awareness, we begin to have choices
> And break the cycle.

As a child in my family I was a hero. In my adult life, this translated into being so busy that I was exhausted and my life was unmanageable. As an adolescent, I was a scapegoat who rebelled. As an adult, this translated into me being "tough"—smoking wasn't going to hurt me. Both roles may have worked for a while, but they nearly destroyed me. My emotional recovery began when I started to see the automatic patterns and then develop healthier choices.

There can be no choices without awareness; please allow the time and energy necessary to develop awareness. The following exercise can help.

Exercise: A Different, Healthy Approach to Roles

Remember to *stop.*
Take three slow, deep breaths.
Take your time as you complete the exercise.

We learn who we are from the role we played in our family. The role is not the person and the person is not the role. At this point, write a statement of what you will *do* differently as a result of learning about the role you've played for many years.

What affirmations do you need to practice? Write them on a piece of paper and tape the paper to your bathroom mirror. Repeat them aloud when you see yourself in the mirror. Put a copy on your desk or anywhere else you spend much time. Please don't skip this step. It is important.

As we stop the ritual of smoking to forget ourselves, we begin to develop awareness and clarity. The most basic definition we have of ourselves is that of our sex and gender role. Write a few sentences about how you measure up as a male or female.

As a woman, I've been keenly aware of the changes in female roles during the past twenty years. Only recently, however, have I started to notice the outdated images of "the American man."[52] I believe the years ahead will offer exciting chances for both men and women to redefine ourselves in a healthier way. As the smoke clears we begin to see our choices.

To get a clearer picture of who you believe you are and who you want to become, complete the next exercise.

Exercise: Defining Who You Are

Remember to *stop.*
Take three slow, deep breaths.
Take your time as you complete the exercise.

Be sure to write the first three things that come to your mind when you complete these questions about sex role. Please write your answers on a separate sheet of paper.

When I was a child, I thought men were . . .

Your Story

As an adult, I think men are . . .

When I was a child, I thought women were . . .

As an adult, I think women are . . .

As a man or woman today, which feelings am I comfortable in showing? Does this have anything to do with what I learned as a child about what feelings are acceptable for men and women to express?

To grow emotionally, it is important to feel and express all feelings. If we didn't learn how to identify and express feelings as children, we have a challenge ahead—learning how to identify and express them as adults. It is important not to be critical of ourselves, but to become gentle and patient as we learn to be men and women who can experience and express the complete range of feelings.

The Definition of Success

When we start to look at our definitions of success, we may have to come to grips with perfectionism. Often recovering nicotine addicts gloss over this area. In all-or-nothing style we may say, "Oh, yes, I am a perfectionist," or "Not me, I'm not a perfectionist." We need to take a closer look.

Exercise: Defining Success

> Remember to *stop.*
> Take three slow, deep breaths.
> Take your time as you complete the exercise.

Many of us are perfectionists and, for our recovery to proceed, it's important to be aware of how pervasive this trait is for us and learn to substitute healthier self-statements. (Finish the following sentences on a separate sheet of paper.)

To be a "success" in my family, it was expected that I . . .

To be a "success" today, I expect myself to . . .

Close your eyes and hear the criticisms of you from your parents. List three.

What are your self-critical messages today?

> Automatically, we keep old patterns alive.
> History repeats itself. We re-create our past.
> The first step in changing is to see the pattern.
> With self-awareness, we begin to have choices
> and break the cycle.

What self-critical messages do you say to yourself when you

- make a mistake at work?
- make a mistake in your intimate relationships?
- make a social error (for example, forget a name, etc.)?
- lose control of your behavior (eat or drink too much, act out sexually or in anger, etc.)?

Many years ago, I learned in basic psychology courses that what people say to themselves greatly influences their outlook. When I was smoking I was too "busy" to take the time to actually listen to what I said to myself. When I stopped smoking I started listening and was amazed at how self-critical I was and how often I expected myself to do things perfectly.

Here are some affirmations that I use to help replace my self-critical messages and to reduce my perfectionism. Pick ones that you need. Repeat them several times each day for a couple of weeks, especially when you notice that you are being self-critical.

- It's OK to make mistakes.
- I can risk making mistakes. That's how I learn.
- I don't have to be perfect. I'm fine just the way I am.
- I celebrate my humanity today and won't focus on little things I do wrong.
- Today I let go of irrational guilt about not being perfect.
- As I grow emotionally and spiritually, I release my perfectionism.

As you work on identifying and modifying what you say to yourself, keep these points in mind:

- Listen to the message without criticizing yourself for it. Remember that your perfectionism may have helped you survive as a child.
- Acknowledge your fear and shame.
- Have a soothing talk with yourself. Don't be so hard on yourself.

Your Story

- Give yourself permission to stop trying to be perfect. Here are a few affirmations to improve your self-concept.

  - It's OK to feel my feelings.
  - It's OK to change my mind.
  - It's OK to take care of myself.
  - It's OK to stand up for my rights and to say no.

Now it's time to look at the way we handle compliments.

Exercise: Handling Compliments

> Remember to *stop*.
> Take three slow, deep breaths.
> Take your time as you complete the exercise.

On a separate sheet of paper, list compliments you have received from others. First, list five compliments you received as a child, then five you received as an adult.

When you are complimented today, what do you think and how do you feel? Take the time to write out your answer.

When you are complimented today, what defenses do you use?

____ I minimize and discount: "It's not *that* good."

____ I use self-criticism: "I should have done better."

____ I am sarcastic and put myself or others down with humor: "I'm a real joke."

____ I ignore the compliment and change the subject: "Let's talk about the weather."

> Automatically, we keep old patterns alive.
> History repeats itself. We re-create our past.
> The first step in changing is to see the pattern.
> With self-awareness, we begin to have choices
> and break the cycle.

Here is a list of three affirmations that can help you deal with compliments.

- I can let other people's compliments nurture me.
- I can accept compliments.
- Compliments and praise soften me, criticism hardens. I can practice accepting praise.

In recovery from nicotine addiction, we may start to identify that we are recovering from perfectionism, too! Reading more about perfectionism can help.[53]

Core Issue Five: All-Or-Nothing Thinking and Control

All-or-Nothing Thinking

No happy medium exists for us addicts, only extremes.[54] There are no shades of gray. It's all or nothing, black or white. Regardless of the name we choose for this thinking style, it is lethal to nicotine addicts in recovery. Here are two examples:

- I am either completely in control or completely out of control; or
- I can trust people completely or I can't trust them at all.

We need to practice moderation in recovery. We need to move into a safer and more comfortable middle ground. For addicts, control and trust issues are particularly affected by all-or-nothing thinking.

Control

Nicotine addicts often talk about the need for control: control over feelings, events, people (ourselves and others). When we stop smoking, the fear of being out of control is common. For us, losing control usually means showing feelings.[55] Nicotine has helped us keep feelings buried. When nicotine is removed the feelings begin to emerge.

To understand our fear of loss of control, it helps to examine what we learned about control as a child in our family.[56] Conflicts over control are a major source of fear. Insight comes from connecting the past to the present.

Exercise: Control

These questions will help you gain that insight. (Write your answers to each of the following questions on a separate sheet of paper.)

Remember to *stop.*
Take three slow, deep breaths.
Take your time as you complete the exercise.

What did losing control mean in my family?

Your Story

Who was allowed to lose control in my family?

What did I feel when someone lost control in my family?

Did anyone get hurt (physically or emotionally) when someone lost control in my family?

How do I feel about losing control over my feelings today?

How am I "all-or-nothing" about control?

> Automatically, we keep old patterns alive.
> History repeats itself. We re-create our past.
> The first step in changing is to see the pattern.
> With self-awareness, we begin to have choices
> and break the cycle.

If you remember bouncing from one extreme to another, not being able to find a middle ground, which of the following do you need to keep in mind?

_____ Feelings come and go in a matter of seconds.

_____ Feelings are not actions. They don't hurt anyone.

_____ Losing control doesn't mean I will go so far that I can't come back.

_____ Losing control doesn't mean I will become suicidal or hurt anyone else.

As a recovering nicotine addict, we can learn new ways to think and behave that will enrich our lives.

- Recognize when we think control is all-or-nothing.
- Learn how to identify and express feelings, and recognize that feelings pass quickly.
- Get support from others as we learn how to deal with our feelings.
- Give ourselves gentle and nurturing messages about moderation.
- Remember to say the Serenity Prayer.
- Go to Twelve Step meetings to practice new behaviors.

Accepting our lack of control and powerlessness, while initially frightening, is very beneficial. Realistically, we cannot control most of what happens around us today. We can only control *our* attitude and *our* behavior. If we can yield to each new day with a realistic attitude, our life will run far more smoothly.

This not only frees us to change the things we can but also helps us embrace life, accepting its variety and beauty. Instead of worrying about how to control external events, we can use the time for quiet moments, to get in touch with how we want to live today, to make contact with our inner wisdom and Higher Power, to surrender to the day as it unfolds. There are distinct benefits in finding the difference between what we can and cannot control.

Dealing with our control issues is challenging. But affirmations, as usual, can help.

- I don't have to live in extremes anymore; I can find the middle ground.
- I can give up my efforts to dominate life and still be safe.
- I can flow with the current of life.
- I can give up trying to control other people and events, and focus on the things I can change.
- I can let my feelings come and go freely. Nothing bad will happen to me. Feelings are a wonderful part of me, and I am learning to accept them.

Core Issue Six: Boundaries and Trust

Boundaries

In recovery from nicotine addiction, we need to learn more about boundaries. A *boundary* is simply a limit. Boundaries between people tell us where one person stops and another begins. We must be aware of our boundaries if we are to learn who we are.[57]

We all have physical, emotional, and spiritual boundaries. When we stop anesthetizing ourselves with nicotine, we become acutely aware of them.

Physical boundaries are obvious. We can see the lines on streets, fences around yards, walls in houses, doors in rooms. As individuals, we have physical boundaries, too. We are comfortable at a certain physical distance from another person. That distance may be determined by how safe we feel with the person, how comfortable we feel being close to someone who is angry, needy, etc. When people are in our home or office and use our things, we have different levels of tolerance depending on who the person is and whether permission was granted. When we stop smoking, the smoke screen that obscured our physical boundaries is cleared and we become more sensitive to them.

Our emotional boundaries contain *our* feelings, as opposed to the feelings of others. When we stop smoking we may find we are very sensitive to other people telling us how we *should* feel. We feel angry when someone tells us that our emotions should be different. Our anger tells us that someone has invaded our emotional territory. This may be a relapse cue to pick up a cigarette, unless we're prepared to say: "I understand you may feel differently, but this is the way I feel." Making this statement is one part of defining our boundaries, the line between where other people stop and we start, the line that was blurred by smoke for many years.

Spiritual boundaries define our belief in a Higher Power, as distinguished from the beliefs of others. When we stop smoking we have a greater sensitivity to what is true spiritually for us, and we may feel angry when someone tries to impose beliefs on us. Once again, we have to be careful that anger does not lead us to light up, as it did thousands of times in the past when our boundaries were violated. Rather, that anger is a cue to assert ourselves by simply stating: "I know that is what you believe and I think your beliefs are fine, but mine are different from yours."

If you are in a relationship with someone who doesn't respect your physical, emotional, or spiritual boundaries you have some work to do. Be true to yourself. If you need additional help, get it. Go to therapy, join a support group. Get what you need. Don't smoke over it.

To learn more about our boundaries, let's complete a few exercises.

Exercise: Boundaries

Remember to *stop.*
Take three slow, deep breaths.
Take your time as you complete the exercise.

Look around the room you are in, if you are inside, and write down all the physical boundaries you see (for example, doors, curtains, walls). Look out a window and note some boundaries outside, too.

Close your eyes and imagine you are in a bubble that serves as a boundary around you. What is the bubble made of? Imagine its size, shape, and color. (Since there is no longer smoke in that bubble, it is easier to see clearly.) How big does that bubble have to be to protect you from the various people in your life? Open your eyes and list on a separate sheet of paper the bubble descriptions and how they changed according to whom you were seeing in the image.

Close your eyes again and imagine sharing your thoughts and feelings with someone important in your life. Now imagine this person's response. Does the person accept what you say or does she or he tell you what you *should* think and feel? Does this person try to change you?

If you can't say no you can't establish healthy boundaries.[58] If you don't have healthy boundaries, you can't have a healthy relationship. *No* is a complete sentence. Only *you* know when *no* is right for you. List the people who refuse to take your *no* for an answer. If you need help in saying *no* and having it taken seriously, I recommend you see a therapist. This is an essential step in your recovery.

Boundary work is crucial in recovery. Here are some strategies to follow:

- Use your feelings to identify your boundaries. Anger and shame are signs your boundaries may have been invaded.
- Watch how other healthy people set boundaries, and see if their methods can work for you.
- Make a list of boundaries that you would like to work on, and ask Twelve Step support people for help on how to establish and maintain healthy boundaries.
- Recognize that you will probably feel guilty when you start saying no and doing boundary work. Guilt doesn't have to mean you are doing something wrong. It may mean you are doing something unfamiliar. Stop and ask yourself: *Am I being true to myself by saying no?* If the answer is yes, then do it. Ask for feedback from your Twelve Step support group, and know that feeling guilty comes with the territory of doing something unfamiliar. Guilt for saying no will diminish when you become more familiar with being true to *yourself.*
- Give yourself credit. Allow yourself to take risks and make mistakes. Get support from others in your new learning.

- Remember that it feels uncomfortable to do boundary work, especially with the people we love the most. But to repeat, if we don't have boundaries we can't possibly have healthy relationships! Establishing boundaries is a loving thing to do.

To help us establish boundaries use the following affirmations.

- My space, time, and feelings are important, and I can say no to people who don't respect them.
- I have the right and the duty to myself to refuse participation in *any* activity that violates me, regardless of how that refusal upsets others.
- I deserve to have my boundaries respected.
- It is my duty to protect my boundaries: physical, emotional, and spiritual.

Trust

Smoking isolates us from others. When we stop we reclaim our feelings and begin to know ourselves better. Then we are ready to begin developing trust in ourselves and in others.

Trust is built slowly, a little at a time. We risk a little and stop to see what happens. Then, if it seems safe, we risk a little more—not in an all-or-nothing way. We do not trust ourselves completely right away, nor do we trust others immediately.

The feedback our feelings give us, which informs our decisions, is clear and unmedicated. A Twelve Step group is a great place to practice these new skills. While reading is beneficial and therapeutic, all the reading we could possibly do won't take the place of practice: risk, wait, and see; if safe, risk again. We listen to our own feedback and the input of others. It's simple, but not easy! Use these affirmations to help develop trust.

- I can relax my tight grip on life and learn to listen to my inner wisdom; I can trust that my Higher Power is in charge.
- I am learning to trust myself as I follow my own thoughts and feelings.
- As I find out what is right for me, I am learning to trust myself.

Core Issue Seven: Inability to Play

Most nicotine addicts haven't the foggiest idea how to play in a spontaneous and healthy way. Play is not serious competition. It's not compulsive activity. Nor is it self-destructive, impulsive, controlling, demanding, or manipulative. Play is spontaneous and fun.[59] To play means to let go with trust: trust that we are acceptable human beings even if we sometimes make fools of ourselves. It's OK to play and risk appearing foolish. But this is hard for the self-conscious nicotine addict who is not medicated.

When we stop smoking and stop force-feeding poisonous gas to our spontaneous, playful center, we are free to experiment with play. We need help, though. Play is free motion and fun, without justification. Compulsive activity and competitive sports don't fit in. The mood must be light and the spirit creative.

Laughter gives us a great workout. Our abdomen, chest, and shoulders contract as our heart rate, breathing, blood pressure, and temperature increase. When the laughter subsides, our heart rate and blood pressure dip below normal. Laughter also stimulates our *endorphins* (the body's natural pain-relieving chemicals). We see evidence of how play and laughter may reduce depression, stress, and a variety of physical problems, in addition to being just plain fun!

As you stop gassing yourself, you can lighten up and begin to enjoy play. In the following exercise, you'll get a chance to look more closely at your history of play.

Exercise: Play

Remember to *stop.*
Take three slow, deep breaths.
Take your time as you complete the exercise.

Complete the following two sentences on a separate sheet of paper.

As a child, this is the way I played:

When I play today I . . .

List on a separate sheet of paper people you know who seem to enjoy playing. Include some thoughts about asking them for help as you learn how to play.

List ways you can play during the next week.

Please remember that learning to play may not come easily. If it seems awkward, begin with just a short period of play. Gradually

Your Story

increase the time you spend playing until a satisfying balance of work and leisure activities is achieved.

Try these affirmations to help develop your ability to play.

- Humor is an important part of my life. I can let go and laugh.
- When I laugh I am alive and in touch with my Higher Power and my spirit of joy.
- I can play and have fun without being self-destructive.
- I can stop being constantly busy and enjoy my leisure time.

Core Issue Eight: Stress Management

As infants we required nourishment, safety, and love. We reduced tension with food and touch. Soon we learned we could reduce stress through self-stimulation such as babbling, rocking, and sucking.[60] As we matured, some of us may have substituted cigarette smoking for thumb sucking as a way to deal with tension.

We all need stress in our lives. Without it, life would be dull and unchallenging. Too much stress, however, seriously affects our well-being. In our addiction, we believed smoking helped us cope with stress. In fact, it numbed us so we couldn't feel our feelings and identify our needs to make healthy decisions. As a result, we may have actually increased our stress. The disease lied to us. The disease told us smoking helped us cope. Our stress, however, just grew and we smoked more. We knew little about relaxation and play as ways of reducing stress.

During my many years of smoking, I lost any natural ability to relax. I began to learn meditation and deep-breathing exercises, but this wasn't enough for me. Then I started to have regular appointments for therapeutic massage[61] and my ability to relax improved immensely. Now that my body *knows* how to feel relaxed, it's easier to return to that state with a few deep breaths. Today I continue those massage sessions and consider them one of the most crucial parts of my self-care program. I recommend regular use of massage as a stress-reduction technique.[62]

Let's look at how we can cope better with stress today.

Exercise: Stress

Remember to *stop.*
Take three slow, deep breaths.
Take your time as you complete the exercise.

If we meet certain basic needs we can deal more effectively with stress. Use this checklist to see what you are now doing for yourself and what areas you may be neglecting. (Note: The time frames given in parentheses are suggested. Other time frames may work better for you. The important thing is to find a program that you can maintain, one day at a time, for the rest of your life.)

I am meeting my needs for

____ a reasonable diet (proper nutrition three times daily).

____ cardiovascular exercise (twenty minutes to one hour, three times a week). Note: See a doctor for a complete physical before embarking on a new exercise program.

____ relaxation exercises (twenty minutes, three times a week).

____ inspiration periods (one hour, three times each week).

____ recreation periods (one hour, three times each week).

____ sleep (six to eight hours each night).

____ physical touch (hugs, safe nonsexual massages).

Affirmations can help reduce stress. Try some of these.

- I can quiet my thoughts and find that still, quiet place within me.
- I let the tension flow out of all my muscles and open myself to peace.
- For this moment, I can be free of all tension and experience calm.
- Calmness is the healing power that helps me through the day.

Core Issue Nine: Intimacy

Smoking cigarettes is a major destroyer of intimacy in relationships.[63] As smokers, we provide ourselves with instant intimacy.[64] The problem is that the intimacy is not with a person but with the smoke we take into our body. As we smoke alone we become more and more isolated.

Nicotine medicates feelings that are absolutely necessary for intimacy. It can medicate feelings until the emotional life is destroyed. When smoking stops, feelings return and we begin to rekindle the trust, hope, and closeness we lost in our addiction. Since we have greater access to who we are, we can bring more of ourselves to relationships.

As the smoke clears, sensuality and sexuality begin to improve, too. Genital blood flow increases.[65] Erections and orgasms improve in recovery; the sexual closeness that follows the emotional closeness stands to improve greatly. Also, our sensitivity to taste and smell increases. Thus, we have the capacity for higher levels of stimulation. Our improved capacity for sexual performance, coupled with an increase in sensual pleasures, invite us to bring more of our energy to our intimate relationships.

To be healthy, a relationship must support clear thinking; the safe sharing of feelings and spirituality; physical health; and sexual vulnerability. This is in contrast to the relationships we have in our addiction, which are characterized as conflict-ridden and de-energized, or merely as relationships of convenience.[66]

To get a better grasp on your intimacy issues, let's complete the following exercise.

Exercise: Intimacy

Remember to *stop.*
Take three slow, deep breaths.
Take your time as you complete the exercise.

Put a check mark by areas you need to develop in your intimate relationships as you progress in recovery from nicotine addiction:[67]

_____ Allowing space and alone time for my partner and for me

_____ Checking out feelings and thoughts with my partner; stopping the guessing and mind-reading

_____ Agreeing to discuss differences, and, when we get stuck, to ask for help from a therapist or friend instead of rehashing old territory

_____ Focusing on finding my self-worth from within and not relying on my partner for it

_____ Having patience with myself and others; relationships take time, shared interests, and common experience

_____ Sharing the words *I love you* and feelings of appreciation for my partner

Here are some statements of direct communication that you can practice with your partner.[68] Which ones will you practice?

_____ This is what I think or feel.

_____ This is what I am hoping or wishing from you.

_____ This is what I think you might be thinking or feeling or needing.

_____ This is what I can do for or will give to you.

_____ This is what I won't do for or won't give to you.

_____ This is what I will accept or take from you.

_____ This is what I won't accept or take from you.

Here are some listening skills you can practice in your relationship.[69] Put a check mark by the ones you need to develop.

_____ Making a commitment to listen without distraction (TV, reading)

_____ Waiting for my partner to finish his or her message before I speak

_____ Using my thinking skills to supplement my listening, not replace my listening (mind-reading)

We may confuse true intimacy with *addictive relationships,* which are characterized by intensity without substance.[70] We feel euphoric and infatuated but do not think clearly or cope with our feelings and act responsibly. Addictive relationships are passionate but not safe. They are based on unrealistic fantasies, not reality. It is not self-caring to have addictive relationships. They provide emotional clutter that recovering nicotine addicts don't need.

To support intimacy, consider using some of these affirmations.

• I am attracted to safe people who are physically, emotionally, and spiritually available for intimacy.
• I can accept the challenge of intimacy as I learn to trust myself.
• I will not be smothered or lose myself as I become intimate.
• I am not a victim nor a rescuer as I enter an intimate relationship.

Intimacy takes effort. (Excellent resources are available to help you learn more about intimacy.[71]) It is new to be honest and open with our partner, dealing in a straightforward and unclouded way. When we were active in our nicotine addiction, this way of relating was not possible. As we recover we have a reprieve from the fatal disease of nicotine addiction. Our relationships have a second chance, too!

Core Issue Ten: Emotional Self-Care

Emotional self-care is essential in recovery from nicotine addiction. Its opposite is self-centeredness. *Self-centered people* are usually shallow. They try to control and manipulate others for their own needs. *Self-caring people* have great concern for others, but they do not take care of others at their own expense. They have healthy boundaries for and realistic expectations of themselves and others.

Charlotte Kasl, Ph.D., has devised "guidelines for codependent sobriety"[72] that were written for codependent women, but I believe they apply to many nicotine addicts. Many of these guidelines have been helpful in my recovery.*

Be willing to know what you know. Or, be willing to feel whatever is inside you; or, be willing to know whatever is true for you. One woman used the phrase "I am willing to do what it takes to find my soul."

Learn to listen inside. Once you are determined to find out who you really are, you can proceed to the next step, listening. There are many approaches to listening. My favorite is to start by taking a quiet time to be aware of your breathing, your insides, and how you feel.

Don't make "fix it" statements. Codependents often attempt to smooth things over when people are upset. They quash other people's anger and expressions of strong feelings because they are afraid of their own. Let people be upset.

Stop telling stories that could be titled "What He (She) Did to Me." This keeps you in a victim role. Women often tell lengthy stories about what others did to them in an attempt to have friends reinforce their sense of powerlessness. They often tell the story with great surprise even if the person has done the same thing a thousand times. The unspoken goal is to have a friend say, "Yes, he sure is a jerk. Poor you, it's really terrible what you go through." Blaming others creates dense energy and is one of the greatest blocks to recovery.

---

*The guidelines that follow are excerpted from *Women, Sex, and Addiction: A Search for Love and Power* by Charlotte Kasl. Copyright © 1989 by Charlotte Kasl. Reprinted by permission of Ticknor & Fields, a Houghton Mifflin Co., and by permission of Houghton Mifflin and the author.

Stop giving reasons for everything you do. Stop using the word *because,* except to say "because I feel like it." Codependents tend to feel they have to justify themselves and build a case for what they think or do. You need to learn to say, "I want to go to that movie." Period. Not, "I want to see that movie, because it would be good for me" (or "because I read an excellent review," or "because Judy said it was really great"). You don't have to bring in an army of reasons to support your stand. If you want to go, just say so. You've got the right.

Take your emotional temperature after visiting various people in your life. After you spend time with someone take a density-to-light reading. On a scale of one to ten, density to light, how do you feel before and after? Become aware of what brings light feelings into your life and what brings dense feelings. Write them down and keep a journal. This can be with statements such as, I feel ____when I spend time with ____, or I feel ____when I ____. List the lightness score along with the feeling.

Change the question Will they like me? *to* Will I like them? Most codependents walk into a party or gathering trembling and thinking, *Will anyone like me? Do I look all right?* This puts a person in a victim role. Instead, ask yourself, *Whom would I like to talk to here?* The reality about gatherings is that sometimes you meet people you click with and sometimes you don't, and it's really no big deal.

Pay attention to behavior, not words. Codependent women are easily seduced by words. But talk is cheap; behavior is the true measure of a person.

Learn to walk through fear. Codependent women say they can't do something hard because they are afraid. Who isn't? Ask yourself what the fear is really about. Remember, too, that you can do things even though you are afraid.

Stomachaches usually signify anger. If you are talking about someone or an event and your stomach suddenly hurts, it is usually anger churning up. The impulse is usually to double up. Do just the opposite. Stand erect and breathe into the feelings. Stomp and swing your arms. Sometimes I ask, "Who are you sick of? Who do you want to throw up on?" Imagine moving the energy up from your stomach into your throat and out into words.

Your Story

Sometimes it helps to put your hand on your stomach and imagine breathing the feelings up.

Protect yourself. When codependent women are being harmed or attacked they tend to want to analyze the situation rather than take cover. To illustrate the point, I often ask clients, "If you are standing under a window and someone starts to dump garbage on top of your head, what do you do?" There is often a long pause. Many people reply tentatively, "Ask them to stop?" instead of the appropriate response, which is, "You get out of the way. You move." Who cares *why* when you're getting covered with garbage.

Become powerful rather than being righteous and superior to others. The codependent high is being righteous and judging others as wrong, stupid, or jerks. It is tough to give up because this superior stance brings a feeling of power. When you feel righteous, jealous, or want to prove someone else wrong, ask yourself, *What's really true? Am I jealous? Am I afraid I could never be on my own?* To confront these truths and give up being righteous is to get to the core of codependency.*

---

*Excerpts from *Women, Sex, and Addiction: A Search for Love and Power,* by Charlotte Kasl, 333–44, Copyright © 1989 by Charlotte Kasl. Reprinted by permission of Ticknor & Fields, a Houghton Mifflin Company, and by permission of Houghton Mifflin and the author.

SUMMARY

An emotional self-care program consists of all the items in this chapter. Place a check mark beside each item that you are working on in your recovery.

_____Identify my compulsive behaviors and begin a program of recovery.

_____Pay attention to my defenses so that I use them less automatically.

_____Instead of smoking, identify and express my feelings in a healthy, assertive manner.

_____Avoid blame, self-pity, and self-righteousness.

_____Avoid extremes and all-or-nothing thinking. Start aiming for the midrange.

_____Develop trust in myself and others.

_____Recognize my boundaries and maintain them with others.

_____Remember that *no* is a complete sentence.

_____Laugh and express joy. Play and have fun with friends.

_____Use stress-reduction techniques instead of smoking.

_____Experience intimacy and tenderness in my relationships with other people.

_____Go for therapy to help process feelings and, if needed, to work through unresolved grief.

_____Accept reality. Focus on what people do, not what they say.

_____Stop trying to control and fix others. Give less advice and fewer explanations. Stop apologizing for being who I am.

_____Protect myself from abusive and destructive relationships. If I am stuck and cannot leave or protect myself, seek professional help.

CHAPTER 4

Spiritual Recovery

ALTHOUGH I DIDN'T REALIZE IT *for years, I have been on a spiritual search most of my life. I used to call it a scientific and philosophical quest for understanding and "control." Back then, I used nicotine to medicate my feelings of inadequacy and insecurity, as well as any other feelings I rejected (anger, loneliness, etc.). When I stopped smoking I began to peel back the layers of defenses and compulsive behaviors to learn who I am under the pretense. In my journey, I have learned that I am not self-sufficient and in control. With that acceptance, I found what I was searching for all along: serenity, courage, and strength to gently accept myself and others. I couldn't achieve any of this when I was struggling in my addiction and battling daily for self-sufficiency and control.*

Significant mutilation of the spirit is the result of any addiction: nicotine is no exception. In recovery I started to recognize nicotine addiction as a gift. I realized that I started out with a sense that something was missing; I searched for a substance to fill the void. Nicotine was the drug I used. In recovery I moved from external fixes to an internal search for wholeness. Within each of us is a source of wisdom. Putting nicotine down helped me quiet my mind and soul so I could go inside and listen to that wisdom. This is one of the ways I now define spirituality: an inner wisdom.

People who have a strong sense of spirituality appear to be content and at peace, regardless of what goes on around them. They have serenity from within, attempting to live by five guidelines.[1]

- Accept ourselves and the world we live in.
- Have a faith in a Higher Power.
- Have ideals to strive for.
- Assume responsibility for our actions.
- Experience each day fully.

Spirituality can be a powerful force in recovery from nicotine addiction. It is a primary force in healing. Although difficult to define, spirituality is often experienced on a personal level as joy, love, compassion, humility, gratitude, and serenity. These feelings are coupled with a connection to a Power greater than oneself. Therefore, the concept of a Higher Power is an integral part of developing spirituality. But there may be barriers to that development. It is often helpful to examine them.

The Concept of a Higher Power

I was driving alone in my car the day I stopped smoking. It was 4 o'clock on a beautiful Sunday afternoon. Suddenly I realized that I was unable to stop smoking and that a Power greater than myself could help if I asked. So I did. I reached my hand out of my open sunroof and "gave" my obsession with cigarettes to my Higher Power. I knew I had to do my part: not buy cigarettes, not put a cigarette into my mouth, stay away (for a while) from people when they were smoking. The obsession was the part I gave to my Higher Power.

I didn't know if my Higher Power was a benevolent life force in the universe, a higher good that comes from within, a divine principle that gives the universe wholeness and purpose, or some or none of the above. All I knew and all I needed to know was that I was powerless over my obsession. Reaching through my sunroof was a symbolic gesture, a good place to start for me. At that moment, I felt a relief and a peace. No more struggle. No more sneaking around in my addiction. I couldn't escape my Higher Power's presence, nor did I want to. I did my part of not picking up a cigarette, and working a program of emotional and spiritual recovery; my Higher Power did the rest.

This may sound silly, but in the beginning I was afraid my Higher Power would give my obsession back. I needed to begin to work a program of recovery immediately.

I began to examine why I had this curious fear about my Higher Power. I started to recognize that my Higher Power seemed like a loving protective force, but a force that could not be counted on consistently. This came from early childhood. I believed my parents (who were then my Higher Power) were good and wonderful people, but they weren't reliably "there" for me. I needed to let go of that concept, the one I had as a child, in order to make room for the concept of my Higher Power today.

Exercise: Higher Power

Remember to *stop.*
Take three slow, deep breaths.
Take your time as you complete the exercise.

To begin to understand why you have the Higher Power you do, take a separate sheet of paper and list the heroes you had as a child.[2] They can be religious figures, family members, characters from history, books, or movies. After each name, write why this person was special to you as a child and whether you still hold this figure in high esteem today.

Now describe in writing the "God" you believed in as a child. Was God like a childhood hero or like one of your parents?

Draw a picture of you and your childhood God.

Now draw a picture of what you would like your Higher Power to be today. Include both you and your Higher Power in the drawing. If you like, use a big sheet of paper. Take your time. This is important work.

Automatically, we keep old patterns alive.
History repeats itself. We re-create our past.
The first step in changing is to see the pattern.
With self-awareness, we begin to have choices
and break the cycle.

Now take your time to answer these questions:

If I am saying good-bye to "the God of my childhood," where am I in the process? If "the God of my childhood" is being replaced by my growing sense of a Higher Power, in what stage of grief am I now?

____ Denial
____ Anger
____ Bargaining
____ Sadness
____ Acceptance and letting go

If you are stuck in any stage of grieving, some of the following barriers may be responsible. Put a check mark by the ones that apply to you.

_____ I blame my childhood God for not providing what I needed.

_____ I have a negative concept of God from my childhood (such as a God who is cruel, punishing, unforgiving, unavailable, distant, nonexistent, etc.).

_____ I believe that science and spirituality are not compatible.

_____ I am in an active addiction or have codependent obsessions. (This means that a substance or another person is, essentially, my Higher Power.)

_____ I am depressed.

_____ I find it hard to delay gratification and to accept responsibility for my actions.

_____ I lack a daily program for spiritual recovery.

Just when I think I know how things are going to happen, my Higher Power surprises me with a new twist of events and I learn something new about myself and others. This often seems like playfulness on the part of my Higher Power. It's then that I smile, inside and out, and remember who is really in charge. There are many ways I experience my Higher Power: loving moments with family and friends, times of gentle laughter with loved ones, cute antics of a pet or other sweet critter, and the list goes on.

What are some of the delights that touch your playfulness?

It may be helpful to write a letter to your Higher Power to begin discussing where you are in your relationship. After completing the letter, it's good to share the letter with members of your support system. Sharing the letter helps you to process the experience and can provide you with insight and growth. Take the time to write a letter to your Higher Power. See what insight arises.

What surprised you the most in your letter? What did you learn?

When I was smoking, my primary search for love and protection was directed toward my cigarettes. Everything else was secondary. Whether I wanted to admit it or not, cigarettes were my Higher Power.

During the last few years I have felt connected to my Higher Power. In this connection, I have felt loved and safe, and my self-esteem and self-worth have grown. The alienation I felt as a smoker is gone.

A spiritual awakening may occur through rapid conversion experiences, but it usually happens slowly and gradually. The changes are slight, and often, barely visible. Then we begin to realize that we are starting to feel good about ourselves and are enjoying our lives. This is only the beginning of spiritual awakening. As the process continues, a feeling of well-being starts to unfold. It is often called "serenity." It is characterized by not being hurried or preoccupied.[3] Serene people do the best they can and let go of the rest. They are relaxed as they take an active part in life, enjoying themselves with faith, humility, hope, and love. In recovery we start to identify ourselves as "serene," at least part of the time.

Prayer and Meditation

God grant me the serenity
To accept the things I cannot change,
The courage to change the things I can,
And the wisdom to know the difference.

The Serenity Prayer is very valuable to recovering nicotine addicts. As a psychologist, I call this prayer a "useful cognitive coping tool."[4] As a nicotine addict, I call it a lifesaver. We need to accept that we cannot change the fact that cravings for cigarettes will come and go. We *cannot* control the fact that we get cravings. We *can* control our response to the craving by not picking up a cigarette.[5]

In our active addiction, smoking a cigarette naturally followed the craving. In recovery, *not* smoking a cigarette follows the craving. The wisdom to know the difference between what we can and cannot change makes all the difference in recovery.

The Big Book[6] describes daily prayers that are useful. Basically, these prayers ask for personal guidance and the acceptance of reality ("Thy will be done").

In the morning, it's helpful to preview our plans for the day, turning to our Higher Power (inner wisdom, God of our understanding, etc.).

- Ask for inspiration, intuition, and guidance in making decisions.
- Ask that we be guided away from self-pity, selfishness, and dishonesty.

At night, before going to sleep, it's helpful to review the day's activities.

- Recognize where we need to make changes and amends (but guard against worry, obsessions, or getting overcome with remorse or self-criticism).
- Ask our Higher Power for forgiveness and guidance in the future.
- Turn everything over to our Higher Power until morning.

In addition to these prayers from the Big Book, I have other forms of prayer and meditation that are helpful in my recovery. I'd like to share them with you.

In the morning, I meditate for ten to twenty minutes. Here's what I do:

- I close my eyes and breathe slowly and deeply.
- I repeat a mantra (the sound I use is "sher-ring") silently in my mind—over and over.
- I return to my mantra every time a thought intrudes, always returning gently and softly, without effort or judgment.
- When finished, I slowly open my eyes and move my hands and feet gradually.
- I resume my morning activities with a sense of calmness and alertness.

During the day, when a problem arises, I find it useful to take the following steps:

- Slow down and breathe deeply.
- Say the Serenity Prayer.
- Accept what I cannot change.
- Feel grateful for the calmness I feel and the energy I've conserved by not burning out on what I cannot change.
- Turn to my inner wisdom for guidance on action I need to take, asking my Higher Power for intuition to know the way.

Many of us have used these prayers or meditations, in some form or another, before we stopped smoking. When we are no longer medicated by nicotine, however, I believe we can experience greater clarity with our inner wisdom and a stronger connection with our Higher Power.

I don't consider myself a religious person, by conventional definition. But my spiritual life is very important to me in my recovery from nicotine addiction. I spend considerable time each day nurturing this part of my life. It's worth every minute. I feel less rushed and have more energy when I am grounded in reality, using the Serenity Prayer and meditations to accept what is.

Exercise: Spiritual Journey

Remember to *stop.*
Take three slow, deep breaths.
Take your time as you complete the exercise.

Meditation books have been an important part of my recovery.[7] Write on a separate piece of paper what types of prayer and meditation are helpful to you.

Think about how and why you pray, if you do, and focus on ways you use prayer to nurture your spiritual growth. Take the time to write your thoughts here. Share them with another person who is also on a spiritual journey.

Conscious Contact with Your Higher Power

This contact is often only a prayer or affirmation away. Affirmations about safety, protection, and well-being are an important part of spiritual recovery. Choose the affirmations that comfort you and repeat them often.

- My Higher Power is always with me.
- My Higher Power is as close as my breath.
- All is well. I can let go.
- I am never alone.
- I have everything I need.
- I am cared for and protected.
- I am safe and loved.

The Twelve Steps and Addiction

The original Twelve Step program is Alcoholics Anonymous (AA). AA began in June 1935 in Akron, Ohio, with two men (a physician and a stockbroker), Dr. Bob and Bill W. They were helped by Dr. William D. Silkworth, a New York alcoholism specialist.

AA is not a religious organization but the role of spirituality is central. (Psychologists may call spirituality "values clarification.")[8] This becomes clear in some of the tenets of the Oxford Groups, which follow, on which AA was based.[9]

- Each person completes a moral inventory.
- Character defects are shared with others.
- Amends are made for harm done.
- Helpfulness to others is necessary.
- The belief in a Power greater than oneself is important. (In AA the Higher Power may be God, *Good Orderly Direction* as a lifestyle, AA group members, Creative Intelligence, or "Spirit of the Universe underlying the totality of things.")[10]

AA plays a crucial role for people recovering from alcoholism. It is a highly effective, twenty-four-hour-a-day, seven-day-a-week communication and support system. AA helps people establish and maintain sobriety; it enhances all areas of their lives. Members rehearse new and healthier thoughts and behavior, strengthen new values and norms, and improve their self-esteem.

There are many Twelve Step programs, all based on AA's Steps and Traditions. All Twelve Step programs promote two important qualities: honesty and spirituality.[11] Some of these programs are listed on pages 118–119.

Before I stopped smoking I read materials from Alcoholics Anonymous and related what I read to my nicotine addiction. I knew I was powerless over cigarettes. There was no way that I could control my smoking. I could not smoke just one cigarette. I fought a battle each day to try to exert my willpower over those little rolls of tobacco, but I was powerless then and I'm powerless now. I can't smoke just one. I'm an addict, just like the alcoholic described in the Big Book.[12]

My life was unmanageable, just like the alcoholic's. My body was deteriorating. I gasped for breath as I walked up stairs. I spent a fortune to maintain my habit, and I sneaked around to smoke so people I respected wouldn't see me. I was tied to the cigarette on the phone, in the car, and nearly everywhere else. If I tried to stop for any period of time, the craving for another cigarette took hold and I was helpless until I had one. This is no different from the hell known to alcoholics. I did things I didn't like and became a person I didn't like.

Exercise: The Enabler and the Provoker

I read that alcoholics have friends and family who, inadvertently, enable them in their drinking.[13] I could apply these ideas to nicotine addiction. See if anyone in your life is playing these roles today.

- *The Enabler.* Enablers want us to stop smoking and believe that they can get us to stop. They don't think we can do it without their help. The enabler may be a friend or a professional such as a physician, therapist, or minister. Enablers become as compulsive about their attempts to get us to stop as we are about our compulsion to use cigarettes. Enablers, although well-meaning, don't help. Often they inadvertently strengthen our denial. They may prevent us from coming to grips with our own self-destruction. Write on a separate sheet of paper who the enablers are in your life today.

- *The Provoker.* Provokers are upset by our smoking and try to force us to change. They may be martyrs, guilt trippers, or just unbearable nags. The more hassle they give us, the more we focus on them, and the more we make excuses so we don't have to deal with our own behavior. Who are the provokers in your life?

It may help if the enablers and provokers in our lives read about detachment and enabling. Al-Anon has developed many excellent materials to help loved ones deal with the alcoholic. These materials can be applied to smoking, too. If someone loves you and wants to help you deal with your smoking addiction, ask him or her to read Al-Anon materials and learn how to *really* help you.

As I came to realize I was powerless over nicotine and couldn't help myself, I started to believe that some Power greater than myself could help—just like alcoholics who go to AA believe. I stopped trying to control my smoking and surrendered. I didn't know exactly what power was in control of my smoking, but I knew I wasn't and that's all I needed to know at first. I read in the Big Book[14] that other people had gone through the same process I had, although they went through it with alcohol, and they eventually came to believe that they could be restored "to sanity."[15] So I became willing to come to believe it, too. Willingness is all that is required—that's what the Big Book said.

Today there are more materials for nicotine addicts than there were when I was struggling. You may find them helpful.

Your Story

However, I also recommend that you do what I did and read the Big Book. It has been a wonderful help for me. Substitute the word *nicotine* wherever *alcohol* appears. It may not apply in every detail, but I believe you will find profound meaning in much of the book. Take what is useful and leave the rest.

Use Twelve Step Support to Recognize When the Addiction Is Talking

Nicotine addiction says crazy things to us. We have to learn to recognize when the addiction is talking and substitute a healthier recovery response. (Psychologists call this "cognitive restructuring.") Support systems, like Nicotine Anonymous, are good places to learn the difference between the words of the addiction and the words of recovery. Here are some examples:

The addiction says:	*Recovery says:*
I am under a lot of stress; a cigarette will relax me.	Nicotine increases my heart rate, blood pressure, and adrenaline level.
One cigarette won't hurt.	One *will* hurt.
I can't stop forever.	I just need to not smoke for this minute only. The urge lasts only five to ten minutes. I can wait it out.
I'll get fat.	I won't get fat if I eat healthy, well-balanced meals.
Why stop now? I failed before. I'll just smoke later.	Now is all I have. Yesterday's gone. Tomorrow is not here.

Admitting Powerlessness

It's worth repeating: Recognize that cravings will come and go; recognize that you are powerless over the cravings. You do have a choice, however, about whether you *act* on those cravings. You can acknowledge the craving and let it pass, or you can light up when it comes.

Remember to talk about the cravings. Don't keep them a secret. When you feel like lighting up, go to someone you trust and talk about your feelings. Realize your choices are not about the cravings but about your *actions* in response to those cravings.

Cravings are often triggered by feelings. Feelings pass, whether you smoke in response to them or not. Remember: It does get better.

Surrender! Admit powerlessness whenever you find it. Live by the principle of "letting go." Change what you can. By admitting powerlessness, you can become more open-minded and willing to accept strength greater than your own!

At least in the beginning of your recovery, avoid people, places, and things that were part of your addiction. Remember you are powerless. Avoid the situation. When in doubt: Don't! Avoid trigger situations, particularly in early recovery.

Smokers who have support are more likely to be successful in smoking cessation.[16] Forgive yourself for slips. Get back on track as soon as possible. Shame due to slips is dangerous. Talk about the slip and then let it pass.

Nicotine Anonymous

The Twelve Step organization called Nicotine Anonymous is based on the Twelve Steps of Alcoholics Anonymous.[17] (Nicotine Anonymous World Services can be reached at 2118 Greenwich Street, San Francisco, California, 94123, or by phoning (415) 922-8575. For your own Nicotine Anonymous meeting see the Appendix for *Tips for Gaining Freedom From Nicotine, The Twelve Promises, The Serenity Prayer For Smokers,* and a meeting format.) Here are the Twelve Steps of Nicotine Anonymous.*

1. We admitted we were powerless over nicotine—that our lives had become unmanageable.
2. Came to believe that a Power greater than ourselves could restore us to sanity.
3. Made a decision to turn our will and our lives over to the care of God *as we understood Him.*
4. Made a searching and fearless moral inventory of ourselves.
5. Admitted to God, to ourselves, and to another human being the exact nature of our wrongs.

---

*The Twelve Steps are reprinted and adapted with permission of Alcoholics Anonymous World Services Inc. Permission to reprint and adapt the Twelve Steps does not mean that Alcoholics Anonymous has reviewed or approved the contents of this publication, nor that AA agrees with the views expressed herein. AA is a program of recovery from alcoholism only. Use of the Twelve Steps in connection with programs that are patterned after AA but which address other problems does not imply otherwise.

6. Were entirely ready to have God remove all these defects of character.
7. Humbly asked Him to remove our shortcomings.
8. Made a list of all persons we had harmed, and became willing to make amends to them all.
9. Made direct amends to such people wherever possible, except when to do so would injure them or others.
10. Continued to take personal inventory and when we were wrong promptly admitted it.
11. Sought through prayer and meditation to improve our conscious contact with God *as we understood Him,* praying only for knowledge of His will for us and the power to carry that out.
12. Having had a spiritual awakening as the result of these steps, we tried to carry this message to nicotine users, and to practice these principles in all our affairs.

A First Step Toward Happiness, Honesty

Happiness is a by-product of working the Steps and living life the way we believe is good for us. I used to think I could seek happiness. Now I know it comes as a gift when I am not smoking and when I am living my life to the best of my ability.

Honesty is essential to our recovery, and Twelve Step meetings provide a chance to be honest about who we are in our addiction and recovery. Honesty heals, and other addicts help keep us honest. When another nicotine addict talks about his or her experiences, our defenses go down. We can then get honest with ourselves and start taking the risk of getting honest with others.

Begin a First Step for your own nicotine addiction. It will help break the denial about your powerlessness and unmanageability so that you can develop the motivation to stay stopped.

Exercise: First Step

Remember to *stop.*
Take three slow, deep breaths.
Take your time as you complete the exercise.

To help this process, please answer these questions:

• How did I attempt to control my smoking (switching to low tar, limiting smoking to certain times and places, attending stop-smoking groups, switching to cigars, setting "stop dates" that I couldn't keep, etc.)?

- What events showed my preoccupation with smoking (worrying about stopping, worrying about illness and dying, worrying about how many cigarettes I have left, etc.)?

- What behavior caused me or others physical and emotional pain (smoking in front of nonsmoking loved ones, physical illness caused by or contributed to by my smoking, etc.)?

- What dangerous situations were caused by my smoking (burning holes in things, burning myself or others, rushing home to see if a cigarette is out, dropping a burning cigarette while driving in the car, etc.)?

Use the Steps

Without a spiritual component, recovery cannot happen. Separate religion from spirituality, if religion carries harmful baggage for you. Meditation books can help with daily readings to support Twelve Step progress.[18] Nicotine Anonymous provides the support and fellowship to work the Steps. (If there is no local chapter, start your own.)

Step One
- It helps us see the powerlessness and unmanageability in our lives and to recognize that we cannot control our smoking.
- We cannot have just one, although it is difficult to admit that we are different from people who can smoke socially or from people who do not smoke at all.
- Reality testing is strengthened. We learn to accept the biological factors that limit us.
- We recognize the problem is not outside ourselves, it is not the job, family, stress, etc., that keeps us from stopping. We smoke because we are addicts.
- We learn to stop trying to control what cannot be controlled.
- We realize we have a disease and stop blaming ourselves for smoking.

Steps Two and Three
- They help us discover a belief in a Power greater than ourselves.

Your Story

We learn to rely on that Power for the strength to not smoke.

- At first that Power may be the support of a Nicotine Anonymous group.
- We are encouraged to develop healthy resources and a support system.
- We stop feeling alone and begin to experience serenity.

Let's see what we have so far: Step One says I can't stop smoking myself; Step Two says someone else can help me; Step Three says I'm going to let someone else help me.

It's good to keep a sharp focus on these first three Steps, especially during the first six months of abstinence from nicotine.

Steps Four, Five, Six, Seven, and Ten

- They help us take honest inventory of ourselves.
- We do an analysis, similar to what is done in psychotherapy.
- We learn to admit and deal with our false pride and other "character defects."
- We learn forgiveness is essential for emotional health and spiritual growth.[19]
- Step Ten helps those of us who are perfectionists to tolerate making mistakes.
- Our self-esteem improves.

Steps Eight and Nine

- They help us make amends for the ways we have hurt others and ourselves.
- We begin to reduce the harmful effects of what we did in our addiction.
- Our self-esteem continues to improve.

Step Eleven

- It helps us learn to be more gentle with ourselves as the concept of a nurturing, flexible, loving Higher Power becomes clearer.

Step Twelve

- It helps us continue our personal growth by using the Steps in every area of our lives.
- We learn to accept ourselves and others.
- We define our values and live within them as we develop ourselves as whole physical, emotional, and spiritual beings.

• We learn to help others as a large part of Step Twelve.

Twelve Step Slogans

Slogans from Twelve Step programs are excellent shorthand devices for complicated people who need simple ways to deal with the pitfalls of recovery. Following is an exercise to help you focus on which slogans or ideas you need to practice. Put a check mark by the ones you will practice.

Exercise: Slogans and Other Wisdom

Remember to *stop.*
Take three slow, deep breaths.
Take your time as you complete the exercise.

When I am disappointed by perfectionistic expectations of myself and others:

____ Progress, Not Perfection
____ Easy Does It
____ If I constantly reach for the moon, I miss little miracles.
____ The Serenity Prayer

When I have guilt and shame about smoking:

____ Nicotine addiction is a disease. I am powerless over my disease.
____ I am not to blame for having a disease, but I am responsible for how I respond to my disease.

When I worry and feel fear:

____ Change What I Can, Let Go of the Rest
____ Let Go and Let God

When I feel self-pity and martyrdom:

____ An Attitude of Gratitude
____ Peace of mind depends on conditions inside, not outside, of me.

When I feel overwhelmed:

____ One Day at a Time

____ Easy Does It

____ Don't make mountains out of molehills: No big deals.

____ Keep It Simple; Change What I Can, Let Go of the Rest

When I feel resentful:

____ How important is it?

____ Change What I Can, Let Go of the Rest

____ Anger is OK. It tells us something is wrong, but blame and resentment may lead me to light up.

Other Twelve Step Programs

Recovering nicotine addicts often find we have other issues to deal with, either before or after we stop smoking. These are national resources that can direct you to local meetings.

Alcoholics Anonymous
(212) 647-1680
(consult local phone book for area office)

Adult Children of Alcoholics
World Service Office
P.O. Box 3216
Torrance, CA 90510
(310) 534-1815

Al-Anon
(212) 254-7236
Al-Anon Family Group
  Headquarters
World Service Office
1600 Corporate Landing Parkway
Virginia Beach, VA 23454
(715) 563-1600

Codependents Anonymous
P.O. Box 33577
Phoenix, AZ 55067
(602) 277-7991

Gamblers Anonymous
International Service Office
P.O. Box 17173
Los Angeles, CA 90017
(213) 386-8789

Incest Survivors Anonymous
International Service Office
P.O. Box 17245
Long Beach, CA 90807-7245

Narcotics Anonymous
World Service Office
19737 Nardhoff Place
Chatsworth, CA 91311
(818) 733-9999

National Service Organization of Codependents of Sexual Addicts
9337 B. Katy Freeway #142
Houston, TX 77024
(612) 537-6904

Overeaters Anonymous
International Service Office
P.O. Box 44020
Rio Rancho, NM 87174-4020
(505) 891-2664

Sexual Addicts Anonymous
International Service Office
P.O. Box 70949
Houston, TX 77270
(713) 869-4902
E-mail: Info@saa-recovery.org
www:http//www.saa-recovery.org

If there are no local meetings for you to attend and if you are interested in forming a support group to meet your needs, ask to have materials sent to you and start your own meeting. Place an advertisement in your local newspaper to find other like-minded individuals. Ask for help and do whatever it takes to recover. You are worth it!

Another Option

As an alternative to the Twelve Steps, Charlotte Kasl devised sixteen steps for recovery and empowerment.*

1. We admitted we were out of control with_____and have the power to heal by taking charge of our lives and stop being dependent on others for our self-esteem and security.
2. We came to believe that God/The Goddess/Universe/Great Spirit/Higher Power would awaken the healing wisdom within us if we opened ourselves to that power.
3. We declared ourselves willing to hear the Universe speak its truths into our spirit, to listen and to *act* based upon these truths.
4. We examine our beliefs, behavior, addiction, and codependency in the context of living in a hierarchal, patriarchal culture.
5. We shared with others and the Universe the ways we have harmed ourselves and others, working to forgive ourselves and to change our behavior.
6. We admitted to our strengths, talents, accomplishments, and intelligence, agreeing not to hide these qualities to protect other's egos.

---

*Excerpt from *Many Roads, One Journey* by Charlotte Davis Kasl, copyright © 1991, Charlotte Davis Kasl. Reprinted by arrangement with HarperCollins Publishers and the author.

7. We became willing to let go of our shame, guilt and any behavior that prevents us from taking control of our lives and loving ourselves and others (such as making excuses for others, analyzing other people, rationalizing why we stay in destructive relationships, using fear as an excuse for not making changes, etc.).

8. We made a list of all people we have harmed and a list of all people who have harmed us, and became willing to clear out all negative feelings between us whenever possible.

9. When appropriate, we took steps to clear out all negative feelings between us and other people, by making amends and sharing our grievances in a respectful way.

10. By speaking the truths about our perceptions, beliefs and feelings whenever appropriate, we daily affirm that we see what we see, we know what we know, and we feel what we feel.

11. We promptly admit to mistakes and make amends when appropriate, but we do not say we are sorry for things we have not done and we do not take responsibility for, analyze, or cover up the mistakes and shortcomings of others.

12. We seek out situations, jobs, and people that affirm our intelligence, perceptions, and self-worth and avoid situations or people which are hurtful, harmful, or demeaning to us.

13. We take steps to heal our physical body, organize our lives, reduce stress, and have fun.

14. We seek, through prayer, meditation, and honest relationships with others, the ability to listen to our inward calling and develop the will and wisdom to follow it.

15. We grow in awareness that we are sacred beings, interrelated with all living things and, when ready, take an active part in helping the planet become a better place for all people.

16. We accept the ups and downs of life as natural events that give us lessons for our growth.[20]

Spiritual Self-Care

To continue the spiritual progress, we need a plan and discipline. What am I willing to *do* for my spiritual recovery?

Exercise: Spiritual Progress

Remember to *stop*.
Take three slow, deep breaths.
Take your time as you complete the exercise.

As you review the following list, put a check mark by the goals you will set for yourself. In recovery from nicotine addiction, my daily spiritual program consists of my willingness to

____ express gratitude for life's gifts.

____ acknowledge a Power greater than myself.

____ pray, meditate, or both, read inspirational material, etc.

____ live in the present, unhurried and not preoccupied.

____ practice compassion and forgiveness for myself and others.

____ acknowledge humility in not having the "right" answers.

____ laugh and express joy; play and have fun.

____ enjoy art and music; notice miracles in nature.

____ transform loneliness into quiet and peaceful solitude.

____ experience intimacy and tenderness in my relationships with other people.

____ use the Serenity Prayer to experience a sense of well-being when I turn it over.

____ attend Twelve Step meetings and work a spiritual program in those groups, in my religious community, etc.

SUMMARY
- Mutilation of the spirit happens in nicotine addiction.
- Developing a relationship with our Higher Power is an integral part of spiritual recovery.
- Examining childhood beliefs about God and religion are helpful in clarifying the beliefs we now hold as adults.
- When we recognize the crazy things our addiction tells us, we can start to substitute healthier responses.
- Admitting powerlessness over our addiction and the unmanageability of our lives is a crucial first step in recovery.
- Nicotine Anonymous and other Twelve Step programs are valuable to us.
- Using Twelve Step slogans and tools are powerful in our recovery.
- Spiritual self-care is essential for our continued growth and development.

Checklist for Physical, Emotional, and Spiritual Self-Care

Physical

____ Maintain adequate nutrition with three meals daily and snacks (as needed).

____ Sleep six to eight hours each night.

____ Exercise fifteen to twenty minutes a day, three times a week.

____ Follow a daily personal care routine.

____ Abstain from alcohol and other drugs.

____ Use only a minimum of sugar and caffeine.

____ Receive weekly therapeutic massages.

____ Balance work and leisure activities.

____ Maintain regular physical and dental checkups.

Emotional

____ Identify my compulsive behaviors and begin a program of recovery.

____ Pay attention to my defenses so that I use them less automatically.

____ Instead of smoking, identify and express my feelings in a healthy, assertive manner.

____ Avoid blame, self-pity, and self-righteousness.

____ Avoid extremes and all-or-nothing thinking. Start aiming for the midrange.

____ Develop trust in myself and others.

____ Recognize my boundaries and maintain them with others.

____ Remember that *no* is a complete sentence.

____ Laugh and express joy. Play and have fun with friends.

____ Use stress-reduction techniques instead of smoking.

____ Experience intimacy and tenderness in my relationships with other people.

____ Go for therapy to help process feelings and, if needed, to work through unresolved grief.

____ Accept reality. Focus on what people do, not what they say.

____ Stop trying to control and fix others. Give less advice and fewer explanations. Stop apologizing for being who I am.

____ Protect myself from abusive and destructive relationships. If I am stuck and cannot leave or protect myself, seek professional help.

Spiritual

____ Express gratitude for life's gifts.

____ Acknowledge a Power greater than myself.

____ Pray, meditate, or both, read inspirational material, etc.

____ Live in the present, unhurried and not preoccupied.

____ Practice compassion and forgiveness for myself and others.

____ Acknowledge humility in not having the "right" answers.

____ Laugh and express joy. Play and have fun.

____ Enjoy art and music. Notice miracles in nature.

____ Transform loneliness into quiet and peaceful solitude.

____ Experience intimacy and tenderness in relationships with other people.

____ Use the Serenity Prayer to experience a sense of well-being when I turn it over.

____ Attend Twelve Step meetings and work a spiritual program in those groups, in my religious community, etc.

Nicotine Anonymous Materials*

The Serenity Prayer For Smokers[1]

God grant me the serenity
To accept the things I cannot change . . .

As smokers trying to stop smoking, we cannot change the craving for cigarettes, but even if we can't change the craving, we can accept it. The truth is that until we can accept our craving for cigarettes, we will not stop smoking. Lighting another cigarette is what we do if we decide we cannot accept the craving!

It's that simple: If you want a cigarette and you will not accept the craving, then you will surely light a cigarette. Or maybe you will have "one puff" to get you through, but even one puff is "not accepting" the things that you cannot change.

Accepting the craving does not mean we want the craving or like it. Accepting it means, first, recognizing the craving for what it is: a strong desire, physical or psychological, *not a need*, for a cigarette. That's all. We do not fight this craving; rather we look at it, letting it be, not getting panic stricken or feeling sorry for ourselves, but saying, "Yes, I really am craving a cigarette right now."

We do not practice self-deception and try to trick ourselves into thinking we don't want to smoke. This is an honest

---

*For literature, meeting schedules, or other information, write Nicotine Anonymous World Services, 2118 Greenwich Street, San Francisco, CA 94123, or call (415) 922-8575. *The Serenity Prayer For Smokers* and *The Twelve Promises* are copyright 1988 by Nicotine Anonymous World Services, San Francisco. *Tips For Gaining Freedom From Nicotine* is copyright 1989 by Nicotine Anonymous World Services. All are reprinted with the generous permission of Nicotine Anonymous World Services.

program. Nor do we try to hate the habit (or ourselves) so much that we quit. No, we cannot make ourselves stop smoking, but we *can* live with the craving, and so we pray for . . .

The courage to change the things I can . . .

The thing that we can change is our unwillingness to live, even for a short time, with the craving for the next cigarette. We can, with God's help and the support of the group, change our old way of dealing with craving, and we deal with it in a new way: We become willing to live with the craving; we no longer light a cigarette to get rid of the pain of craving. Our lighting up shows that we have not accepted what we cannot change and have not acted with the courage to change the things we can. Of course, living with a craving is hard, sometimes very hard, but you are not alone—with God's help you can do it. That is what this Serenity Prayer is all about.

So we ask God to help us accept the craving, and then we ask God to give us the courage not to take care of this craving—as we have always done—by smoking one more cigarette. Thus, we need the strength to accept the craving, and the courage not to light up . . .

And the wisdom to know the difference.

The wisdom we ask for here is to become aware of the difference between our old way of handling the discomfort of craving in the past (by compulsively lighting up) and the new way of dealing with cravings: accepting the craving until it passes, uncomfortable though we may be for a few moments.

The strength and courage to live as ex-smokers with this discomfort does come if we ask for it, even though it may take time. What we receive is not raw will power, but Power that comes from God, from the group, and from our inner-most self! The power that we want is actually *love!* It is only with this kind of power that we can become ex-smokers and receive a new life free from nicotine addiction.

The reason we did not become ex-smokers years ago is that we chose not to live with the craving. Every time we craved a cigarette, we gave in and smoked it. And kept on hoping that in some magic way a day would arrive when the craving would disappear or we would find an absolutely painless way to stop smoking. That day never came. Each of us kept using our favorite rationalizations or excuses for lighting up, our own justification for not living with the craving. And we kept on craving and smoking, craving and smoking, year after year. But now we can change all that: The moment we can accept what is—"I want to smoke"—and face it with the courage God gives us, we can say, "I choose not to handle this craving by smoking a cigarette"— then we become ex-smokers!

If you continue to smoke even though you say this prayer, then say it again, and again, and keep on saying it while you reflect what it means to you, a smoker. Eventually it will work. It will not work if you are not sincere, but if all you can do at first is to say the prayer without believing it, then at least do that! Some time may be needed for you to receive the power to live with the discomfort that comes from craving without lighting up, but eventually it will come. In time, the craving will diminish greatly, and someday, we trust, it will disappear altogether. If you have a slip, however, and you light one up, accept yourself reverently and say the prayer again the next time!

Remember, it really is not the stress, frustration or even the craving that causes us to have another cigarette, but rather our lack of strength to deal with the craving. That strength comes from God, from the group, and from your own healthy inner self! May God be with you now!

—J.S.

The Twelve Promises: Introduction[2]

The program of Nicotine Anonymous is taken directly from the "Big Book" of AA with the permission of Alcoholics Anonymous World Services, Inc.

AA assures us that if we are willing to go to any length and to work the twelve steps that the program suggests, certain promises will come true in our lives. These promises are found throughout the entire "Big Book," but there is a specific reference to the promises found on pages 83–84.

We believe that these same 12 promises will come true for us if we are painstaking, thorough, fearless and honest in working the 12 steps as they apply to Nicotine Anonymous.

Nicotine Anonymous is not a religious program but rather a spiritual program which teaches us to live by certain principles such as patience, tolerance, kindliness, love, honesty and humility. Having had a spiritual awakening as the result of working the 12 steps, we try to carry this message to other nicotine users and to practice these principles in all our affairs.

Nicotine Anonymous is not a program to teach us how to quit using nicotine but rather a program that will teach us how to start living without nicotine.

The Twelve Promises

1. *We are going to know a new freedom and a new happiness.* Until a person who has been addicted to nicotine for any length of time becomes free of this drug, only then can he realize the freedom that he has achieved. Once we are willing to work the 12 steps and ask for help from a power greater than ourselves, we are at last able to be free of the bondage which has controlled us. For us freedom means no longer being a slave to a substance which has controlled our actions, thoughts, ideas, and lives. Once we have obtained this freedom from bondage, we can commence to enjoy the happiness for which we had always been searching.

2. *We will not regret the past nor wish to shut the door on it.* Experience is one of the most valuable assets in anyone's life, and it is this experience that we can share with others who are trying to break this same addiction. We will not wish to shut the door on our past for the same reason. By keeping our past as an open door, we will be able to be helpful to others, which is now our primary purpose. It has been proven once the obsession for nicotine has been lifted from us, our past will turn out to be the greatest asset we possess.

3. *We will comprehend the word serenity.* Calmness and tranquility seem to be two of the finer qualities of life for which we were always searching. Serenity can be equated to inner tranquility and calmness during times of stress and uncertainty. When we are trying to calm ourselves or adapt to stressful situations by inhaling the highly toxic drug nicotine into our system, adverse effects always occur. After the obsession for nicotine has passed and the residuals of the drug have been cleared from our system, unexpected results begin to happen. A calmness and a tranquility begin to appear in our lives as we have never experienced before.

4. *We will know peace.* The dictionary defines peace as freedom from war or hostilities. During our years of using nicotine,

most of us were at war with ourselves knowing that we were practicing a routine in our daily lives with which we were unhappy, but not knowing how to eliminate it. Once we have called upon a power greater than ourselves to help us, we find that the obsession to use nicotine will be removed and we can, at last, know peace. The war we have been fighting with ourselves comes to an end with calmness and peace. Our bodies no longer tell us that we can't use nicotine while our minds continue to tell us we cannot *not* use it.

5. *No matter how far down the scale we have gone, we will see how our experience can benefit others.* Even if our nicotine use has taken us near to the gates of death before we become able or willing to accept the Nicotine Anonymous program, our past will again be an asset to others. As noted in the second promise, we will want to hang onto our past experiences so that we will be able to share them with others as our contribution to their recovery. In Nicotine Anonymous we concentrate not so much on all our differences as on our similarities associated with the prolonged use of nicotine. When we share our stories with others, they will be able to say: "Yes, that happened to me."

6. *That feeling of uselessness and self-pity will disappear.* During our final days of nicotine use, most of us had acquired a feeling of worthlessness. We felt that we were weak because we couldn't give up "such a habit." Once we found ourselves unable to quit, we felt that it was useless to even try because we had failed so many times already. We started feeling sorry for ourselves and continued to smoke over these feelings of uselessness and self-pity. We have come to believe that nicotine use is not merely a bad habit; it is an addiction as strong as an addiction to any of the illegal drugs. Here we found that once we asked for the willingness to get honest with ourselves and to surrender our hopelessness and helplessness to a power greater than ourselves we were on our way to recovery. We were also on our way to leading a healthy and useful life—nicotine free.

7. *We will lose interest in selfish things and gain interest in our fellows.* As we grow in the fellowship of Nicotine Anonymous, we find ourselves practicing such principles as patience, tolerance, kindness and love. We find ourselves becoming more interested in the welfare of others. As nicotine users, we

found that we were basically very selfish and self-centered people. Our concern for our personal use of nicotine was always uppermost in our minds. Usually we did not think of the other fellow's rights or preferences, but used nicotine whenever or wherever it pleased us, caring less whether or not it pleased others. Now we find ourselves being more concerned for the rights, feelings and desires of others.

8. *Self-seeking will slip away.* When we seek things only for our selfish ends, we tend to be very selfish people. We discovered that, while using nicotine, we thought mainly of ourselves and of our own interests. Most of our decisions were made with our own interests in mind. We seldom thought of other people before we thought of doing something for ourselves. As self-seeking disappears, we continue to gain more calm and peace within ourselves.

9. *Our whole attitude and outlook upon life will change.* Selfishness, resentment, self-centeredness, fear, anger, and other negative emotions ruled our lives. If we were to live and enjoy life without nicotine, we would have to change our attitudes and outlook upon life. Just how were we going to be able to do this? By working the 12 steps, most of us were able to see that it was our attitudes that needed to be changed if we were to enjoy the promises. When we apply these newly found principles to our lives, our entire attitudes changed. When we were willing to change our attitudes, our whole outlook on life changed.

10. *Fear of people and of economic insecurity will leave us.* Many of us were starting to feel uneasy around other people because of our uncontrollable urge to use nicotine. Our simply being places where nicotine was *not* used was no longer acceptable. We were also spending money on our addiction which could have been used much more effectively for other things. When we were able to adjust to our new way of living life without nicotine, we found that we were accepted more readily by other people, we smelled better, we looked better and we had much greater self-esteem. We also found that we were spending our money much more wisely.

11. *We will intuitively know how to handle situations which used to baffle us.* It seemed that even some of the simplest of tasks, such as making a telephone call, taking a break, leaving a church or library, driving a car or just waking in the morning

couldn't be done without the use of nicotine. As we gave up the use of nicotine, one day at a time, and became willing not to use nicotine just for today, we also found that we were doing many of our daily routines with hardly even a thought of nicotine. Now we handle these simple tasks without the use of nicotine.

12. *We will suddenly realize that God is doing for us what we could not do for ourselves.* Our faith and belief in a power greater than ourselves, who will help us be free of our need to use nicotine, is the power by which we can live. As our nicotine-free days continue to pass, we notice that good things are happening in our lives for which we can take little credit. We believe that this power, greater than ourselves, is causing life to happen just as it is supposed to happen. Our only responsibility is to show up on a daily basis and to do the things that are suggested.

Tips For Gaining Freedom From Nicotine[3]

This brochure contains practical suggestions for people new to not smoking and new to Nicotine Anonymous. Used in conjunction with regular attendance at meetings and with practice of the Twelve Steps, they can help you live happily, free of nicotine.

1. *It's not as hard as you think.* Once you begin to be honest with yourself and to look at the facts about smoking, it will become a pleasure to remove this addiction from your life.

2. *Square off with your smoking habit.* Look at it and size it up. Ask yourself exactly what it is doing for you; then ask yourself what it is not doing for you. You can begin with your hair and work your way down to the tips of your toes. It is a medical fact that smoking affects every organ in the human body in a harmful way.

3. *Look at quitting cigarettes* as giving yourself a gift—a very big gift. You are giving yourself a better quality of life and, very possibly, a longer life. You are giving yourself a healthier body. You are giving yourself more self-esteem. Wrap all this in a package and look at it for the gift it really is, then *"Go for it!"*

4. *Set a date. Make a commitment.* Give it a try. Remember, it is all right if you don't succeed at first. Just keep trying. The only way you can lose is by ceasing to try.

133

5. *Don't look at it as if you are giving up something.* This makes it seem too much like a loss. What you are really doing is tossing something out of your life that has done you harm and doesn't belong here anymore. You are throwing away pure garbage. No longer are you going to allow your lungs to be a resting place for nicotine and tars.

6. *Always keep a positive attitude.* After all, this is one of the most positive things you've ever done. Stay away from negative people and worrisome situations.

7. *Quit for yourself.* Even though your family and loved ones will benefit tremendously from your quitting, it is you that will benefit most.

8. *Treat giving up smoking with the respect it rightly deserves.* Become willing to go to any lengths to remove it from your life. If you are not willing, try praying for the willingness. This usually works.

9. *Look up the word* nicotine in your dictionary and write down the definition in big letters: *A poisonous alkaloid used as an insecticide.* Put it where you can see it.

10. *Don't say "I'll take my chances" and continue to smoke.* They are not ours to take. We didn't give ourselves life and we don't have the right to "take our chances" on giving it away. That is up to God.

11. *Don't fool yourself* by saying you have too many pressures in your life right now to give up cigarettes. If you are smoking, this in itself is a pressure—a very great pressure. Every day is a gamble and your life is at stake. By getting nicotine out of your life, other things will become easier to handle. You will feel better about yourself and you will have more energy. You will have accomplished something more meaningful than all the money and material objects you could ever acquire. You will have given yourself what no one else could give you. You will no longer have the pressure of being a smoker.

12. *Don't use the excuse* that you might gain weight to justify your continuing to smoke. Even if you do gain a little, the fact that you will be more active and will get more exercise should counteract any weight gain. Remember, overeating, not stopping smoking, causes weight gain.

13. *Plan to do things* that will keep your mind off smoking. Sometimes our minds can be our worst enemies. They will tell us that we need a cigarette for just about any reason that

is handy at the time. By doing things like going to the movies and sitting in the non-smoking section, munching on popcorn or sucking on a lollipop, we can keep our minds occupied and get a break. Go to museums and other places where smoking isn't allowed. Swimming is a good idea, too.

14. *Quit smoking one day at a time* and think only about the part of the day you are in. "I am not going to smoke before noon." "I am not going to smoke before three o'clock." Sometimes just do it one hour at a time. This is a lot easier than trying to quit forever.

15. *Don't subject yourself to smoky situations.* If you do come into contact with someone who is smoking, just say to yourself, "He is having the cigarette I might be having"; then, be grateful you don't have to have it.

16. *While you are quitting.* Look at it as an investment. Once you have quit for one hour, you have invested this hour in becoming a healthier person. Now, invest one more hour. Continue to add to your investment hour by hour. It will grow and become more valuable as the hours go by. You will begin to see and feel the rewards from this investment more and more. Protect and guard it just as you would a treasure.

17. *Start being kind to yourself.* It is the beginning of a new way of life for you and you are the most important one there. Treat yourself with respect and love and, remember, you are no longer filling your system with poison every few minutes. Breathe the clean air and breathe it deeply. Smell the different and wonderful fragrances. Begin to spend time outdoors close to nature. Many new sensations await you.

18. *Don't get too angry.* If we are angry, our minds tell us we need a cigarette to cope. Until your mind learns that it doesn't need a cigarette to cope, try to avoid situations that might be setting you up. Avoid certain people that may bother you. If there is a lot of tension at work, try to get a few days off. If you can't get some time off, quit smoking on a long weekend. Avoid, as best you can, things like getting stuck in traffic. Use a lot of caution. Anger can be very destructive.

19. *Don't get too hungry.* It is amazing how our minds will tell us that everything's wrong when all we really need to do is eat.

20. *Don't get too tired.* If we are tired, it is easy to become irritated and when we get irritated our minds will tell us that a cigarette will help. Our overall resistance becomes weak and it is easy to say, "Oh well, I guess I'll smoke."

21. *Don't get too lonely.* It is good to know some people who are going through the same thing. By going to Nicotine Anonymous meetings you can get phone numbers of such people.
22. *You can remember these four things by the word* HALT. Hungry, angry, lonely, tired. If you feel you need a cigarette, check. Make sure you are not experiencing any of these.
23. *Don't get too bored.* It is hard to just sit and not smoke. Keep busy. Find things to do that you enjoy. Bike riding, hiking, swimming, exploring new places, trying new restaurants. This is the time to indulge yourself.
24. *Have something to fidget with.* We are accustomed to holding a cigarette; being without one might leave our hands at a loss. Get a small rubber ball or a yo-yo. Play dough is good also, or a piece of clay.
25. *Have something handy to put in your mouth.* Life Savers are good, or any slowly dissolving candy. Beef jerky and lollipops help, too. Avoid fattening foods like cookies. They don't last long and they fill you up. Experiment while you are still smoking to see what will relieve the craving. If Life Savers work, then stock up. Just a note of caution: don't use this type of substitute on a long-term basis.
26. *If you always* have a cigarette with a cup of coffee, stop drinking coffee before you quit smoking.
27. *Don't drink alcohol* while you are quitting. Once alcohol is in your system your defenses will diminish greatly.
28. *Remember that the discomfort* you experience in the first 2 weeks will definitely come to an end and you will never have to go through it again.
29. *Frequently give yourself a pat on the back.* What you are doing isn't easy by any means. It takes a lot of guts to try to quit smoking.
30. *If you are feeling pain* from withdrawal, let it become a lasting memory to serve as a reminder of exactly how strong the drug nicotine is and how hooked you really are.
31. *Remember, every minute* you were sucking on cigarettes they were sucking on you. They were sucking the very life out of you. Don't let them have anymore.
32. *Avoid the self-pity trap.* If we begin to feel sorry for ourselves, our minds will tell us that we deserve a cigarette to make us feel better.
33. *Remember, if you just keep trying, you will win.* It is good against evil and the odds are stacked in your favor.

34. *Before quitting, plan your activities* for the first few days after you quit. This way you won't have to make too many decisions while you are withdrawing. At first, making decisions may be hard without a cigarette.

35. *If you are not going to quit right away, then start cutting down.* If you smoke 2 packs a day and you cut back 1 cigarette a day for a month, you will be down to just 10 cigarettes a day. Some people, however, have found cutting back to be almost as hard as quitting.

36. *Drink lots of liquids* to help flush the poison out of your system. Orange juice is good because smoking depletes the vitamin C content in our bodies.

37. *Remember, it is the first cigarette that gets you started.* It takes only one. This is the one you don't have. You can always put off lighting that first one for a little while. Don't fool yourself and think you can start and stop at will. You can't. Many people have tried this and gone on to live the rest of their lives never to experience freedom from nicotine again.

38. *Frequently remind yourself* about the differences you have noticed in yourself. Things like: Your breath no longer smells like a dirty ashtray. Your teeth are beginning to lose their yellow color and look bright and clean. Your fingers aren't stained from tobacco. That sickly sounding smoker's cough is disappearing. Your senses of smell and taste are returning. Your complexion is beginning to improve. Your general attitude about yourself is better because you are beginning to really care about yourself.

39. *Give it away.* Whenever you have a chance to give your experience, strength and hope to another smoker, use it. This act of giving will ensure your chances for staying off nicotine and give strength to your program. There is much reward in helping someone else to gain freedom from this harmful substance.

40. *Have a follow-up program.* Don't assume it is over because you have made it through a couple of weeks. Nicotine is very cunning. Continue to attend Nicotine Anonymous meetings. If there are no meetings in your area, help to get one started. It is very simple. All you need are a place to meet and a few interested people.

41. *When you want to smoke, read this list of tips.*

Participation Meeting: Nicotine Anonymous

Preamble[4]

Ours is a fellowship of women and men who share our experience, strength, and hope with each other that we may solve our common problem and help others to recover from their nicotine addiction. The only requirement for membership is a desire to stop smoking. There are no dues or fees for membership; we are self-supporting through our own contributions. We are not allied with any organization. We do not wish to engage in any controversy, endorse nor oppose any causes. Although there is no organizational affiliation between Alcoholics Anonymous and our fellowship, we are based on the principles of AA. Our primary purpose is to stay healthy and help other smokers achieve freedom from our nicotine addiction.

How It Works[5]

Rarely have we seen a person fail who has thoroughly followed our path. Those who do not recover are people who cannot or will not completely give themselves to this simple program. . . . They are naturally incapable of grasping and developing a manner of living which demands rigorous honesty. . . . There are those, too, who suffer from grave emotional and mental disorders, but many of them do recover if they have the capacity to be honest.

Our stories disclose in a general way what we used to be like, what happened, and what we are like now. If you have decided you want what we have and are willing to go to any length to get it—then you are ready to take certain steps.

At some of these we balked. We thought we could find an easier, softer way. But we could not. With all the earnestness at our command, we beg of you to be fearless and thorough from the very start. Some of us have tried to hold on to our old ideas and the result was nil until we let go absolutely.

Remember that we deal with a smoking addiction—cunning, baffling, powerful! Without help it is too much for us. But there is One who has all power—that One is God. May you find Him now!

Half measures availed us nothing. We stood at the turning point. We asked His protection and care with complete abandon.

The Twelve Steps[6]

Here are the steps we took, which are suggested as a program of recovery:

1. We admitted we were powerless over nicotine—that our lives had become unmanageable.
2. Came to believe that a Power greater than ourselves could restore us to sanity.
3. Made a decision to turn our will and our lives over to the care of God *as we understood Him.*
4. Made a searching and fearless moral inventory of ourselves.
5. Admitted to God, to ourselves, and to another human being the exact nature of our wrongs.
6. Were entirely ready to have God remove all these defects of character.
7. Humbly asked Him to remove our shortcomings.
8. Made a list of all persons we had harmed, and became willing to make amends to them all.
9. Made direct amends to such people wherever possible, except when to do so would injure them or others.
10. Continued to take personal inventory and when we were wrong promptly admitted it.
11. Sought through prayer and meditation to improve our conscious contact with God *as we understood Him,* praying only for knowledge of His will for us and the power to carry that out.
12. Having had a spiritual awakening as the result of these steps, we tried to carry this message to nicotine users, and to practice these principles in all our affairs.

Many of us exclaimed, "What an order! I can't go through with it." Do not be discouraged. No one among us has been able to maintain anything like perfect adherence to these principles. We are not saints. The point is, that we are willing to grow along spiritual lines. The principles we have set down are guides to progress. We claim spiritual progress rather than spiritual perfection.

Our understanding of nicotine addiction and our personal adventures before and after make clear three pertinent ideas:

(a) That we were addicted to nicotine and could not manage our own lives.

Appendix B

(b) That probably no human power could have relieved our addictive behavior.
(c) That God could and would if He were sought.

Now, we'll read the Twelve Traditions. _____, would you like to begin?

The Twelve Traditions[7]

1. Our common welfare should come first; personal recovery depends on Nicotine Anonymous unity.
2. For our group purpose there is but one ultimate authority—a loving God as He may express Himself in our group conscience. Our leaders are but trusted servants; they do not govern.
3. The only requirement for Nicotine Anonymous membership is a desire to stop smoking.
4. Each group should be autonomous except in matters affecting other groups or Nicotine Anonymous as a whole.
5. Each group has but one primary purpose—to carry its message to the smoker who still suffers.
6. A Nicotine Anonymous group ought never endorse, finance or lend the Nicotine Anonymous name to any related facility or outside enterprise, lest problems of money, property and prestige divert us from our primary purpose.
7. Every Nicotine Anonymous group ought to be fully self-supporting, declining outside contributions.
8. Nicotine Anonymous should remain forever nonprofessional, but our service centers may employ special workers.
9. Nicotine Anonymous, as such, ought never be organized; but we may create service boards of committees directly responsible to those they serve.
10. Nicotine Anonymous has no opinion on outside issues; hence the Nicotine Anonymous name ought never be drawn into public controversy.
11. Our public relations policy is based on attraction rather than promotion; we need always maintain personal anonymity at the level of press, radio and films.
12. Anonymity is the spiritual foundation of all our Traditions, ever reminding us to place principles before personalities.

Remember, there is no "good time" to quit smoking except for right now. Quitting is individual. Use what you learn here and file the rest for future reference. Also, your attempts to quit smoking are a practice in stopping for good and represent a sincere desire to stop smoking. Make cessation of smoking a cause for celebration and challenge.

Now, it's time for the daily readings. Who would like to volunteer?

I'll pass around a sign-up sheet for future meetings. Also, a phone list is being passed around. Please use this list.

When you are called on please state your name and the condition of your addiction. I would like to start participation with _____. (Or, if you prefer, ask if anyone wishes to participate.)

End the meeting at 8:00 P.M.

It is time to stop the participation. What you have heard here tonight in the group meeting, what is said member to member, should be held in the strictest confidence. What you hear here, let it stay here.

There are no dues or fees, however, we do pass the basket to cover our expenses. If you are new or a visitor, please feel no obligation to contribute. [After baskets are passed] Are there any announcements that would be of interest to the group?

We have a nice way of closing.

I would like to thank the participants. After a moment of silent meditation and a deep breath I would like to ask _____ to lead us in the Lord's Prayer.

Endnotes

Introduction

1. *Alcoholics Anonymous,* 3rd ed. (New York: Alcoholics Anonymous World Services, 1976), 58–59.

2. E. H. Hoffman, C. Blackburn, and S. Cullari, "Five year follow-up study of brief residential nicotine treatment," *Journal of Addictive Diseases* (1997) Vol. 16, 4:18A. (Other publications of this research are in progress.)

Chapter 2: Physical Recovery

1. Council on Scientific Affairs, "The worldwide smoking epidemic: Tobacco trade, use and control," *Journal of the American Medical Association* 263 (1990): 3312–18.

2. R. T. Ravenholt, "Tobacco's impact on the 20th century U.S. morbidity patterns," *American Journal of Preventive Medicine* 1 (1985): 4–17.

3. ————, "Addiction mortality in the United States, 1980: Tobacco, alcohol and other substances," *Population and Development Review* 10 (1984): 697–724.

4. R. Petro, A. D. Lopez, J. Boreham, M. Thun, and C. Health Jr., "Mortality from tobacco in developed countries: Indirect estimation from national vital statistics," *Lancet* (1992) 339:1268–1278.

5. H. Milkman and S. Sunderwirth, *Craving for Ecstasy: The Consciousness and Chemistry of Escape* (Lexington, Mass.: Lexington Books, 1987), 14, 71.

6. A. Wikler, "Dynamics of drug dependence: Implications of a conditioning theory for research and treatment," *Archives of General Psychiatry* 28 (1973): 611–16.

7. E. M. Jellenik, "Phases of alcohol addiction," *Quarterly Journal of Studies on Alcohol* 13 (1952): 673–84; J. R. Milam and K. Ketcham, *Under the Influence: A Guide to the Myths and Realities of Alcoholism* (Seattle: Madrona Publishing, 1981); M. M. Glatt, "Group therapy in alcoholism," *British Journal of Addiction* 54: 2 (distributed by The National Council on Alcoholism, Inc., New York).

8. H. M. Trice and J. R. Wahl, "A rank order analysis of the symptoms of alcoholism," *Quarterly Journal of Studies on Alcohol* 19 (December 1958): 4.

9. L. Kozlowski, D. Wilkinson, D. Skinner, C. Kent, T. Franklin, and M. Pope, "Comparing tobacco cigarette dependence with other drug dependence," *Journal of the American Medical Association* 261 (1989): 898–901.

10. J. R. Hughes, "Nicotine withdrawal, dependence, and abuse," in DSM–IV *Sourcebook, Vol. 1,* edited by T. A. Widiger, A. J. Frances, H. A. Pincus, M. B. First, R. Ross, and W. Davis, Washington, D. C., American Psychiatric Association (1994) 109–116; and J. R. Hughes, "Smoking as a drug dependence: A reply to Robinson and Pritchard." *Psychopharmacology* (Berl) (1993) 113: 282–283.

11. G. A. Giovino, J. E. Henningfield, S. L. Tomar, L. G. Escobedo, and J. Slade, "Epidemiology of tobacco use and dependence," *Epidemiology Review* (1995) 17: 28-2–293.

12. Relapse rates—"Research status report: Nicotine dependency and compulsive tobacco use," Center for Health Communications, Harvard Medical School of Public Health (19 June 1986), 2; nicotine's addictive qualities, and attempts to quit—W. Pollin, "The role of the addictive process as a key step in the causation of all tobacco-related diseases," *Journal of the American Medical Association* 252 (1984): 2874; knowledge of health hazards—Department of Health and Human Services, Public Health Services, *The Health Consequences of Smoking: 25 Years of Progress: A Report of the Surgeon General,* Washington, D.C.: Government Printing Office, 1989 (DHHS publication [CDC] 89-8411); nicotine's addictive properties—N. L. Benowitz, "Medical intelligence: drug therapy"; J. A. Oates and A. J. J. Wood, "Pharmacologic aspects of cigarette smoking and nicotine addiction," *New England Journal of Medicine* 319 (1988): 1318–30.

13. Benowitz, "Medical intelligence"; Oates and Wood, "Pharmacologic aspects," 1318–30.

14. J. E. Henningfield, "How tobacco produces drug dependence," in *The Pharmacologic Treatment of Nicotine Dependence: Proceedings of the World Conference,* J. K. Ockene, ed., 4–5 November 1985 (Cambridge, Mass.: Institute for the Study of Smoking Behavior and Policy, 1986): 19–31.

15. W. A. Hunt, L. W. Barnett, and L. G. Branch, "Relapse rates in addiction programs," *Journal of Clinical Psychology* 27 (1971): 455–56.

16. Department of Health and Human Services, Public Health Services, *The Health Consequences of Smoking: Nicotine Addiction: A Report of the Surgeon General,* Washington, D.C.: Government Printing Office, 1988 (DHHS publication [CDC] 88-8406).

17. R. Hurt and J. Slade, "Beyond Koop: Part one of five," *Professional Counselor* (January/February1990).

18. Solving problems—Benowitz, "Medical intelligence"; Oates and Wood, "Pharmacologic aspects," 1318–30; performing other tasks—K. Wesnes and D. M. Warburton, "Smoking, nicotine and human performance," *Pharmacology Therapy* (1983): 51–61.

19. D. M. Warburton, "The function of smoking," in *Advances in Behavioral Biology*, vol. 31, W. R. Martin, G. R. Vanboon, E. T. Swamoto, and L. Davis, eds.; *Tobacco Smoking and Nicotine: A Neurobiological Approach* (New York: Plenum Press, 1987): 51–61.

20. Benowitz, "Medical intelligence"; Oates and Wood, "Pharmacologic aspects," 1318–30.

21. T. Rustin, "Treating nicotine addiction," *Alcoholism and Addiction* (December 1988), 18–21.

22. Department of Health and Human Services, Public Health Services, *Why People Smoke Cigarettes*, Washington, D.C.: Government Printing Office, revised 1984 (No. 83—50195).

23. Ibid.

24. J. R. Hughes "Nicotine withdrawal, dependence, and abuse," in *DSM-IV Sourcebook, Vol. 1*. Edited by T. A. Widiger, A. J. Frances, H. A. Pincus, M. B. First, R. Ross, and W. Davis, Washington, D.C., American Psychiatric Association (1994) 109–116; and J. R. Hughes, "Smoking as a drug dependence: A reply to Robinson and Pritchard," *Psychopharmacology* (Berl) (1993) 113:282–283.

25. R. Petro, A. D. Lopez, J. Boreham, M. Thun, and C. Health Jr., "Mortality from tobacco in developed countries: Indirect estimation from national vital statistics," *Lancet* (1992) 339:1268–1278

26. Health benefits of quitting—U.S. Department of Health and Human Services, *Health Benefits of Smoking Cessation: A Report of the U.S. Surgeon General*, Washington, D.C., U.S. Government (1990); health consequences of smoking—Department of Health and Human Services, *The Health Consequences of Smoking: 25 Years of Progress*, 89-8411.

27. Benowitz, "Medical intelligence"; Oates and Wood, "Pharmacologic aspects," 1318–30.

28. Health benefits of quitting—U.S. Department of Health and Human Services, *Health Benefits of Smoking Cessation: A Report of the U.S. Surgeon General*, Washington, D.C., U.S. Government (1990); health consequences of smoking—Department of Health and Human Services, *The Health Consequences of Smoking: 25 Years of Progress*, 89-8411.

29. University of California: *Berkeley Wellness Letter* (May 1990).

30. Hurt and Slade, "Beyond Koop: Part one of five."

31. Health benefits of quitting—U.S. Department of Health and Human Services, *Health Benefits of Smoking Cessation: A Report of the U.S. Surgeon General*, Washington, D.C., U.S. Government (1990); health consequences of smoking—Department of Health and Human Services, *The Health Consequences of Smoking: 25 Years of Progress*, 89-8411.

32. National Institute of Health, publication 89-1647 (February 1989).

33. Health benefits of quitting—U.S. Department of Health and Human Services, *Health Benefits of Smoking Cessation: A Report of the U.S. Surgeon General,* Washington, D.C., U.S. Government (1990); health consequences of smoking—Department of Health and Human Services, *The Health Consequences of Smoking: Nicotine Addiction,* 88–8406.

34. Ibid.

35. Menopause—S. M. McKinlay, N. L. Bifano, and J. E. McKinlay, "Smoking and age at menopause in women," *Annals of Medicine* 103 (1985): 350–56; stroke—collaborative group for the study of stroke in young women, "Oral contraceptives and stroke in young women: associated risk factors," *Journal of the American Medical Association,* 231 (1975): 718–22; heart attack—S. Shapiro, D. Stone, L. Rosenberg, D. W. Kaufman, P. D. Stolley, and O. S. Miettinen, "Oral contraceptives, use in relation to myocardial infarction," *Lancet* 1 (1979): 743–47.

36. Osteoporosis—H. W. Daniell, "Osteoporosis of the slender smoker's vertebral compression fracture and loss of metacarpal cortex in relation to post menopausal cigarette smoking and lack of obesity," *Archives of Internal Medicine* 136 (1976): 298–304; cancer of the cervix—Department of Health and Human Services, *The Health Consequences of Smoking: Nicotine Addiction,* 88–8406.

37. Department of Health and Human Services, *The Health Consequences of Smoking: 25 Years of Progress,* 89–8411.

38. J. W. Kikendall, J. Evaul, and L. F. Johnson, "Effects of cigarette smoking on gastrointestinal physiology and non-neoplastic digestive tissue," *Journal of Clinical Gastroenterology* 6 (1984): 65–79.

39. Department of Health and Human Services, *The Health Consequences of Smoking: 25 Years of Progress,* 89–8411; D. P. Kadunce, R. Burr, R. Gress, R. Kanner, J. L. Lyon, and J. J. Zone, "Cigarette smoking: Risk factor for premature facial wrinkling," *Annals of Internal Medicine* 114 (1991): 840–44.

40. R. E. Frye, B. S. Schwartz, and R. L. Doty, "Dose-related effects of cigarette smoking on olfactory function," *Journal of the American Medical Association* 263 (9) (2 March 1990): 1233–36.

41. R. A. Appell, J. T. Flynn, and A. Paris, "Occult bacterial colonization of bladder tumors," *Journal of Urology* 124 (1980): 345-46.

42. Peptic ulcers—Kikendall, Evaul, and Johnson, "Effects of cigarette smoking," 65–79; Blood pressure—C. Dollery and P. J. Brennan, "The Medical Research Council hypertension trial: The smoking patient," *American Heart Journal* 115 (1988): 276–81; pain—"Decreased clinical efficacy of propoxyphene in cigarette smokers," *Clinical Pharmacology and Therapeutics* 14 (1973): 259–63.

43. Passive smoke—U.S. Department of Health, Education, and Welfare, *The Health Consequences of Smoking: A Report of the U.S. Surgeon General,* Washington, D.C., Government Printing Office, 1972 (DHEW publication [HMS] 72-7516); dangers of smoking—Office of Health and

Environment Assessment, *Respiratory Health Effects of Passive Smoking: Lung Cancer and Other Disorders,*" Washington, D.C., U.S. Government Printing Office (1992).

44. Office of Health and Environmental Assessment, *Respiratory Health Effects of Passive Smoking: Lung cancer and other disorders,* Washington, D.C., (1992) U.S. Government Printing Office.

45. Fielding and Phenow, "Involuntary smoking," 1452–61.

46. T. R. Martin and M. B. Bracken, "Association of low birth weight with passive smoke exposure in pregnancy," *American Journal of Epidemiology* 124 (1986): 633–42.

47. G. Mau and P. Netter, "The effects of paternal cigarette smoking on perinatal mortality and the incidences of malformations," *Deutsche Medizinische Wochenschrift* 99 (1974): 1113–18.

48. J. E. Fielding, "Smoking: health effects and control," *New England Journal of Medicine* 313 (1985): 491–98; Fielding and Phenow, "Involuntary smoking," 1452–61.

49. D. T. Janerich, W. D. Thompson, L. R. Varela, P. Greenwald, P. H. S. Chorost, C. Tucci, M. B. Zaman, M. R. Melamed, M. Kiely, and M. F. McKneally, "Lung cancer and exposure to tobacco smoke in the household," *New England Journal of Medicine* 323 (1990): 632–36.

50. S. Glantz, University of California, San Francisco, presentation at World Conference on Lung Health, reported by the Associated Press (21 May 1990).

51. *Berkeley Wellness Letter* (June 1990).

52. Benowitz, "Medical intelligence"; Oates and Wood, "Pharmacologic aspects," 1318–30.

53. J. R. Hughes, "Dependence potential and abuse liability of nicotine replacement," *Biomedical Pharmacotherapy* (1989) 43:11–17.

54. C. T. Orleans, "Understanding and promoting smoking cessation: overview and guidelines for physician intervention," *Annual Review of Medicine* 36 (1985): 51–61.

55. R. C. Klesges, K. D. Ward, and M. DeBon, "Smoking Cessation: A successful behavioral/pharmacologic interface," *Clinical Psychology Review* (1996) 16:479–496.

56. "Model of progression and recovery based on work of E. M. Jellenik's model of alcoholism, Phases of alcohol addiction," *Quarterly Journal of Studies on Alcohol* 13 (1952): 673–84.

57. Withdrawal symptoms—D. K. Hatsukami, J. R. Hughes, and R. W. Pickens, "Tobacco withdrawal: an experimental analysis," *Psychopharmacology* (Berlin) 8 (1984): 231–36; desire to smoke—Benowitz, "Medical intelligence"; Oates and Wood, "Pharmacologic aspects," 1318–30.

58. J. R. Hughes and D. K. Hatsukamis. "The nicotine withdrawal syndrome: A brief review and update." *International Journal of Smoking Cessation* (1992) 1:21–26.

59. National Institute of Health, publication 89-1647 (February 1989).

60. Milkman and Sunderwirth, *Craving for Ecstasy,* 179.

61. Source: K. M. Cummings, G. Giovino, C. R. Jaen, and L. J. Emrich, "Reports of smoking withdrawal symptoms over a 21-day period of abstinence," *Addictive Behaviors* 10 (4) (1985): 373–81.

62. National Institute of Health, publication 89–1647 (February 1989).

63. J. A. Swanson, J. W. Lee, J. W. Hoppe, and L. S. Berk. "The impact of caffeine use on tobacco cessation and withdrawal," *Addictive Behaviors* (1997) 1:55–68.

64. A. H. Oliveto, J. R. Hughes, S. Y. Terry, W. K. Bickel, S. T. Higgins, S. L. Pepper, and J. W. Fenwick. "Effects of caffeine on tobacco withdrawal," *Clinical Pharmacological Therapy* (1991) 50:157–164.

65. J. A. Swanson, J. W. Lee, J. W. Hopp, and L. S. Berk, "The impact of caffeine use on tobacco cessation and withdrawal," *Addictive Behaviors* (1997) 1:55–68.

66. *American Journal of Psychiatry* (November 1997).

67. *Quitting Times: A Magazine for Women Who Smoke,* prepared by the Fox Chase Cancer Center and funded by the Pennsylvania Department of Health, 1987, adapted and published in NIH 89–1647 (February 1989).

68. See P. Goldberg and D. Kaufman, *Everybody's Guide to Natural Sleep* (Los Angeles: Tarcher, 1990).

69. See also M. Davis, E. R. Eshelman, and M. McKay, *The Relaxation and Stress Reduction Workbook,* 2nd ed. (Oakland: New Harbinger, 1982).

70. Benefits of quitting—American Cancer Society, *Dangers of Smoking, Benefits of Quitting and Relative Risks of Reduced Exposure* (1980); body healing—National Institute of Health, publication 89–1647 (February 1989).

71. Withdrawal symptoms, use of clonidine—A. G. Glassman, F. Stetner, T. Walsh, P. S. Raizman, J. L. Fleiss, T. B. Cooper, and L. S. Covey, "Heavy smokers, smoking cessation, and clonidine: Results of a double-blind, randomized trial," *Journal of the American Medical Association* 25999:19 (20 May 1988): 2863–66; Cravings—A. G. Glassman, W. K. Jackson, B. T. Walsh, et al., "Cigarette smoking, smoking withdrawal, and clonidine," *Science* 226 (1984): 864-66; Behavioral counseling and clonidine—L. S. Covey and A. G. Glassman, "New approaches to smoking cessation," *Drug Therapy* (October 1990): 55–61.

72. Nicotine gum—W. Lam, P. C. Sze, H. S. Sacks, and T. C. Chalmers, "Meta-analysis of randomized controlled trials of nicotine chewing gum," *Lancet* 2 (1987): 27–30; behavioral counseling— M. G. Goldstein, R. Niaura, M. J. Follick, et al., "Effects of behavioral skills training and schedule of nicotine gum administration on smoking cessation," *American Journal of Psychiatry* 146 (1989): 56–60; Study on nicotine gum users—P. Hajek, P. Jackson, and M. Belcher, "Long-term use of nicotine

chewing gum," *Journal of the American Medical Association* 260 (1988): 1593–96.
73. *Practice guideline for the treatment of patients with nicotine dependence,* American Psychiatric Association. *1996) 23–28.*
74. Department of Health and Human Services, *The Health Consequences of Smoking: 25 Years of Progress,* 89–8411.
75. R. C. Klesges, A. W. Meyers, and M. E. LaVasque, "Smoking, body weight, and their effects on smoking behavior: A comprehensive review of the literature," *Psychological Bulletin* (1989) 106:204–230.
76. K. A. Perkins, "Issues in the prevention of weight gain after smoking cessation," *Annals of Behavioral Medicine* (1994) 16:46–52.
77. Average weight gain—*Clinical Opportunities for Smoking Intervention: A Guide for the Busy Physician,* National Heart, Lung, and Blood Institute Smoking Education Program, NIH publication 86–2178 (August 1986); increased sugar intake—N. E. Grunberg, "The effects of nicotine and cigarette smoking on food consumption and taste preferences," *Addictive Behaviors* 7 (1982): 317–31; increased sugar intake—S. M. Hall, D. Ginsberg, and R. T. Jones, "Smoking cessation and weight gain," *Clinical and Consulting Psychology* 54 (1986): 342–46; weight gain—Department of Health and Human Services, *The Health Consequences of Smoking: 25 Years of Progress,* 89–8411.
78. N. E. Grunberg, K. A. Popp, and S. E. Winders, "Effects of nicotine on body weight in rats with access to 'junk' foods," *Psychopharmacology* 94 (1988): 536–39.
79. H. Shimokata, D. C. Muller, and R. Andres, "Studies in the distribution of body fat, III. Effects of cigarette smoking," *Journal of the American Medical Association* 261 (1989): 1169–73.
80. Grunberg, Popp, and Winders, "Effects of nicotine," 536–39.
81. Ibid.
82. C. M. McBride, S. A. French, P. L. Pirie, and R. W. Jeffrey, "Changes over time in weight concerns among women engaged in the cessation process," *Annals of Behavioral Medicine,* (1996) Vol. 18 4:273–278.
83. See also J. Brody, *Jane Brody's Good Food Book* (New York: Norton, 1985); J. Kirschmann, *Nutrition Almanac* (New York: McGraw-Hill, 1984); J. Robbins, *Diet for a New America* (Walpole, N.H.: Stillpoint, 1987).
84. K. A. Perkins, L. H. Epstein, B. L. Marks, R. L. Stiller, and R. G. Jacob, "The effect of nicotine on energy expenditure during light physical activity," *New England Journal of Medicine* 320 (1989): 898–903.
85. T. T. Gorski and M. Miller, *The Phases and Warning Signs of Relapse* (Independence, Mo.: Independence Press, 1984).

Chapter 3: Emotional Recovery

1. S. S. Tomkins, "Script theory: Differential magnification of affect," in *Nebraska Symposium on Motivation,* vol. 26, H. E. Howe Jr. and R. A. Dienstbier, eds. (Lincoln, Neb.: University of Nebraska Press, 1979); S. S. Tomkins, "The quest for primary motives: Biography and autobiog-

raphy of an idea," *Journal of Personality and Social Psychology* 41 (2) (1981): 306–29.

2. S. S. Tomkins, *Affect, Imagery, Consciousness,* 4 vols. (New York: Springer, 1962, 1963, 1991, 1992); J. Bradshaw, *Homecoming: Reclaiming and Championing Your Inner Child* (New York: Bantam, 1990).

3. C. L. Whitfield, *A Gift to Myself* (Deerfield Beach, Fla.: Health Communications, 1990).

4. J. Friel and L. Friel, "Uncovering our frozen feelings: The iceberg model of co-dependency," *Focus* (November/December 1987).

5. Core issues originally published in *Healing the Child Within,* 1987 (p. 196) © by Charles L. Whitfield, Health Communications. Also published in *Synopsis of Co-dependence,* 1991, © by Charles L. Whitfield, Deerfield Beach, Fla.: Health Communications. Reprinted by permission of Health Communications and the author.

6. T. L. Cermack and S. Brown, "Interactional group therapy with adult children of alcoholics," *International Journal of Group Psychotherapy,* 32 (3) (1989): 375–89; C. Black, *Repeat After Me* (Denver: MAC, 1985); and H. L. Gravitz and J. D. Bowden, *Recovery: A Guide for Adult Children of Alcoholics* (New York: Simon & Schuster, 1987).

7. Inner child—see J. Bradshaw, *Homecoming;* "Child within"—see Whitfield, *Healing the Child Within;* "Magical child"—See W. Kritsberg, *The ACOA Syndrome* (Deerfield Beach, Fla.: Health Communications, 1986).

8. Kritsberg, *The ACOA Syndrome.*

9. Effective uses of affirmations—W. Kritsberg, *Gifts: Advanced Skills for Alcoholism Counselors* (Pompano Beach, Fla.: Health Communications, 1983); healing and affirmations—R. Lerner, *Daily Affirmations for Adult Children of Alcoholics* (Pompano Beach, Fla.: Health Communications, 1985).

10. P. Carnes, *Contrary to Love: Helping the Sexual Addict* (Minneapolis: CompCare, 1988).

11. J. Friel and L. Friel, *Adult Children: The Secrets of Dysfunctional Families* (Deerfield Beach, Fla.: Health Communications, 1988).

12. E. H. Hoffman, C. Blackburn, and S. Cullari, "Five year follow-up study of brief residential nicotine treatment," *Journal of Addictive Diseases,* (1997) Vol. 16, 4:18A (other publications of this research are in progress); and J. R. Hughes, "Clinical implications of the association between smoking and alcoholism," in *Alcohol and Tobacco: From Basic Science to the Policy: NIAAA Reserach Monograph 30,* edited by J. Fertig and R. Fuller, Washington, D.C. (1995) 171–181.

13. Compulsive behaviors originally published in *A Gift to Myself* (p. 45) 1990 © by Charles L. Whitfield, Health Communications. Reprinted by permission of Health Communications and the author.

14. J. R. Hughes, "Clinical implications of the association between smoking and alcoholism, in *Alcohol and Tobacco: From Basic Science to Policy:*

NIAAA Research Monograph 30, edited by J. Fertig and R. Fuller. Washington, D.C. (1995) 171–181.

15. S. M. Shiffman, "Relapse following smoking cessation: A situational analysis," *Journal of Consulting and Clinical Psychology,* (1982) 50:71–86.

16. R. Hughes. "Clinical implications of the association between smoking and alcoholism," in *Alcohol and Tobacco: From Basic Science to to Policy: NIAAA Research Monograph 30,* edited by J. Fertig and R. Fuller, Washington, D.C. (1995) 171–181.

17. R. Hughes. "Clinical implications of the association between smoking and alcoholism," in *Alcohol and Tobacco: From Basic Science to Policy: NIAAA Research Monograph 30,* edited by J. Fertig and R. Fuller, Washington, D.C. (1995) 171–181; and R. D. Hurt, K. M. Eberman, I. T. Croghan, K. P. Offord, L. J. Davis Jr., R. M. Morse, M.A. Palmen, and B. K. Bruce, "Nicotine dependence treatment during inpatient treatment for other addictions: A prospective intervention trial," *Alcohol Clinical and Experimental Research* (1994) 18: 867–872.

18. Milkman and Sunderwirth, *Craving for Ecstasy.*

19. Ibid.

20. Lerner, *Daily Affirmations.*

21. T. Adler, "Worrywarts suppress healthy reaction to fear," *APA Monitor* (Washington, D.C.: American Psychological Association, October 1990).

22. D. G. Gilbert, F. J. McClernon, N. F. Rabinovich, L. C. Plath, R. A. Jesnsen, and C. J. Meliska, "Effects of smoking abstinence on mood and craving in men: Influences of negative-affect-related personality traits, habitual nicotine intake, and repeated measurements," *Personality and Individual Differences* (In Press) Southern Illinois University, Carbondale, Ill.; M. S. Gold, "The pyschology of smoking," *Professional Counselor* (1996) 29–59; T. M. Piasecki, S. L. Kenford, S. S. Smith, M. C. Fiore, and T. B. Baker, "Listening to nicotine: Negative affect and the smoking withdrawal connundrum," *Psychological Science* (1997) 8, 3: 184–89.

23. See C. Black, *Repeat After Me.*

24. E. H. Hoffman, C. Blackburn, and S. Cullari, "Five year follow-up study of brief residential nicotine treatment," *Journal of Addictive Diseases* (1997) 16, 4:18A. (Other publications of this research are in progress.)

25. Originally published in *Healing the Child Within,* 1987, by C. L. Whitfield, Health Communications.

26. Excerpts from *Women, Sex, and Addiction: A Search for Love and Power,* by Charlotte Kasl, Harper and Row, 1989 (p. 203–4). Copyright © 1989 by Charlotte Kasl. Reprinted by permission of Ticknor & Fields, a Houghton Mifflin Co., and by permission of Houghton Mifflin and the author.

27. See R. E. Alberti and M. L. Emmons, *Your Perfect Right: A Guide to Assertive Living,* 5th ed. (San Luis Obispo, Calif.: Impact, 1990).

28. J. Bradshaw, *Healing the Shame that Binds You* (Deerfield Beach, Fla.: Health Communications, 1988).

29. From "Rediscovering your cycles of power," a workshop given by R. Lerner, 1986.

30. M. A. Fossum and M. J. Mason, *Facing Shame: Families in Recovery* (New York: Norton, 1986).

31. Bradshaw, *Healing the Shame*.

32. Family rules—Fossum and Mason, *Facing Shame;* Lerner, "Rediscovering your cycles of power" workshop; Bradshaw, *Healing the Shame,* 39–40.

33. Lerner, "Rediscovering your cycles of power" workshop; Fossum and Mason, *Facing Shame,* 52.

34. Lerner, "Rediscovering your cycles of power" workshop; Bradshaw, *Healing the Shame,* 52.

35. Bradshaw, *Healing the Shame,* 56; Lerner, "Rediscovering your cycles of power" workshop.

36. See Bradshaw, *Healing the Shame;* H. L. Gravitz and J. D. Bowden, *Guide to Recovery* (New York: Simon & Schuster, 1985); Fossum and Mason, *Facing Shame;* G. Kaufman, *Shame: The Power of Caring* (Rochester, Vt.: G. Schenkman Books, 1980); and *Shame Faced* (Center City, Minn.: Hazelden Educational Materials, 1986).

37. G. Rosellini and M. Worden, *Anxiety and Recovery from Chemical Dependency* (Center City, Minn.: Hazelden Educational Materials, 1990).

38. *Loneliness,* Hazelden Pocket Power Series (Center City, Minn.: Hazelden Educational Materials, 1986).

39. From Elisabeth Kübler-Ross, "The five stages of dying," *Encyclopedia Science Supplement* (New York: Grolier, 1971), 92–97, as well as her many other publications on the stages of dying, death, and grieving.

40. C. Wills-Brandon, *Learning to Say No: Establishing Healthy Boundaries* (Deerfield Beach, Fla. Health Communications, 1990).

41. Resources I find helpful: R. E. Alberti and M. L. Emmons, *Your Perfect Right,* 6th ed. (San Luis Obispo, Calif.: Impact, 1990); and H. G. Lerner, *The Dance of Anger* (New York: Harper and Row, 1987).

42. A. T. Beck, *Cognitive Therapy and Emotional Disorders* (Madison, Conn.: International Universities Press, 1976).

43. L. S. Convey, A. H. Glassman, and F. Stetner, "Major depression following smoking cessation," *American Journal of Psychiatry* (1997) 154, 2:263–265. E. H. Hoffman, C. Blackburn, and S. Cullari. "Five year follow-up study of brief residential nicotine treatment," *Journal of Addictive Diseases* (1997) 16, 4:18A. (Other publications of this research are in progress.)

44. E. H. Hoffman, C. Blackburn, and S. Cullari, "Five year follow-up study of brief residential nicotine treatment," *Journal of Addictive Diseases* (1997) 16, 4:18A. (Other publications of this research are in progress.)

45. G. Humfleet, S. Hall, V. Reus, K. L. Sees, R. Mufloz, and E. Triffleman, "The efficacy of nortriptyline as an adjunct to psychological treatment for smokers with and without depressive histories." (1995) *NIDA Research Monograph*, Vol. 62. In *Problems of Drug Dependence* (1996), edited by M. Adler, Rockville: Maryland National Institute on Drug Abuse, 334.

46. *Practice guideline for the treatment of patients with nicotine dependence,* American Psychiatric Association (1996) 30–31.

47. R. D. Hurt, P. L. Sachs, E. D. Glover, K. P. Offord, J. A. Johnson, L. C. Dale, M. A. Khayrallah, D. R. Schoeder, P. N. Glover, C. R. Sullivan, I. T. Croghan, and P. M. Sullivan, "A comparison of sustained-release bupropion and placebo for smoking cessation," *The New England Journal of Medicine* 337, 17: 1195–1202.

48. L. S. Convey, A. H. Glassman, and F. Stetner, "Major depression following smoking cessation," *American Journal of Psychiatry* (1997) 154, 2:263–265; M. S. Gold, *Tobacco* (1995) Plenum Medical Book Company: New York 77–84; C. Lerman, J. Audrian, C. T. Orleans, R. Boyd, K. Gold, D. Main, and N. Caporaso, "Investigation of mechanisms linking depressed mood to nicotine and dependence," *Addictive Behaviors* (1996) 21, 1: 9–19; G. G. Swan, M. M. Ward, and L. M. Jack, "Abstinence effects as predictors of twenty-eight-day relapse in smokers," *Addictive Behaviors* 21, 4:481–490.

49. J. R. Hughes, "Possible effects of smoke-free inpatient units on psychiatric diagnosis and treatment," *Journal of Clinical Psychology* (1993) 54: 109–114.

50. R. West and P. Hajek, "What happens to anxiety levels on giving up smoking?" (1997) *American Journal of Psychiatry,* 154, 11: 1589–1592.

51. All roles originally published in *The Family Trap*, 1976 © by Sharon Wegscheider-Cruse. Also published in *Choicemaking*, 1986 © by Sharon Wegscheider-Cruse, Health Communications.

52. R. Bly, *Iron John* (Reading, Mass.: Addison-Wesley, 1990). See also J. Lee, *The Flying Boy: Healing the Wounded Man* (Deerfield Beach, Fla.: Health Communications, 1989).

53. M. LeBoutillier, *Little Miss Perfect* (Denver: MAC, 1987); A. Miller, *The Drama of the Gifted Child* (New York: Basic Books, 1981); A. Smith, *Overcoming Perfectionism, the Superhuman Syndrome* (Deerfield Beach, Fla.: Health Communications, 1990).

54. P. Carnes, *A Gentle Path Through the Twelve Steps: A Guidebook for All People in the Process of Recovery* (Minneapolis: CompCare, 1989), 7.

55. Black, *Repeat After Me.*

56. Gravitz and Bowden, *Recovery: A Guide for Adult Children of Alcoholics,* 46.

57. Defining boundaries—M. Beattie, *Beyond Codependency and Getting Better All the Time* (San Francisco: Harper/Hazelden, 1989); learning who we are—C. L. Whitfield, *A Gift to Myself* (Deerfield Beach, Fla.: Health Communications, 1989).

58. C. Wills-Brandon, *Learning to Say No: Establishing Healthy Boundaries* (Deerfield Beach, Fla.: Health Communications, 1990).

59. Whitfield, *A Gift to Myself*.

60. Milkman and Sunderwirth, *Craving for Ecstasy*.

61. D. Juhan, *A Handbook for Bodywork: Job's Body* (Barrytown, N.Y.: Station Hill Press, 1987); S. McGeeney, "Touching adult children of alcoholics," *Massage Therapy Journal* (Summer 1988).

62. Contact the American Massage Therapists Association, 1130 W. North Shore Ave., Chicago, Illinois 60626-4670 [(312)-761-2682] and ask for information about certified massage therapists in your area.

63. S. Wegscheider-Cruse, *Coupleship: How to Build a Relationship* (Deerfield Beach, Fla.: Health Communications, 1988).

64. Fossum and Mason, *Facing Shame*.

65. K. P. Juenemann, T. F. Lue, J. A. Luo, N. L. Benowitz, M. Abozeid, and E. A. Tanagho, "One effect of cigarette smoking on penile erection," *The Journal of Urology,* 138 (August 1987): 438–41.

66. S. Wegscheider-Cruse, *Intimacy and Commitment* (Rapid City, S.D.: Nurturing Networks, 1988).

67. M. Rumsey, *The Recovering Partner: Healing and Intimacy in Your Relationship,* Keep It Simple Series (Center City, Minn.: Hazelden Educational Materials, 1990).

68. R. B. Stuart, *Helping Couples Change: A Social Learning Approach to Marital Therapy* (New York: The Guilford Press, 1980).

69. Ibid.

70. T. T. Gorski, *Addictive Relationships: an Overview* (Hazel Crest, Ill.: The CENAPS Corporation, 1989).

71. M. Scarf, *Intimate Partners* (New York: Ballantine Books, 1987); J. Paul and M. Paul, *Do I Have to Give Up Me to Be Loved by You?* (Minneapolis: CompCare, 1983); M. McKay, M. Davis, and P. Fanning, *Messages: The Communication Skills Book* (Oakland: New Harbinger, 1983); Wegscheider-Cruse, *Coupleship;* Wegscheider-Cruse, *Intimacy and Commitment;* H. G. Lerner, *The Dance of Intimacy* (New York: Harper and Row, 1990); Rumsey, *The Recovering Partner.*

72. Excerpts from *Women, Sex, and Addiction: A Search for Love and Power,* by Charlotte Kasl, 333–44, Copyright © 1989 by Charlotte Kasl. Reprinted by permission of Ticknor & Fields, a Houghton Mifflin Co., and by permission of Houghton Mifflin and the author.

Chapter 4: Spiritual Recovery

1. B. Jackson, *Afire with Serenity* (Center City, Minn.: Hazelden Educational Materials, 1977).

2. *The 12 Steps—A Way Out: A Working Guide For Adult Children From Addictive and Other Dysfunctional Families* (San Diego: Recovery, 1989).

3. *Serenity,* Hazelden Pocket Power Series (Center City, Minn.: Hazelden Educational Materials, 1986).

4. *Innovations in Clinical Practice: A Source Book,* vol. 5, P. A. Keller and L. G. Ritter, eds. (Sarasota, Fla.: Professional Resource Exchange, 1986), 88.
5. *The Serenity Prayer for Smokers* (San Francisco: Nicotine Anonymous World Services, 1988).
6. *Alcoholics Anonymous,* 3rd ed. (New York: Alcoholics Anonymous World Services, 1976), 86–88.
7. *Each Day a New Beginning: Daily Meditations for Women,* Hazelden Meditation Series (New York: Harper/Hazelden, 1982); *Touchstones: A Book of Meditations for Men,* Hazelden Meditation Series (Center City, Minn.: Hazelden Educational Materials, 1986); R. Lerner, *Daily Affirmations for Adult Children of Alcoholics* (Pompano Beach, Fla.: Health Communications, 1985); K. Casey, *If Only I Could Quit: Recovering from Nicotine Addiction* (Center City, Minn.: Hazelden Educational Materials, 1989); M. Chandler, *Gentle Reminders for Co-Dependents* (Deerfield Beach, Fla.: Health Communications, 1989).
8. *Innovations in Clinical Practice,* 83.
9. *Alcoholics Anonymous,* xvi.
10. Ibid., 46.
11. Carnes, *A Gentle Path Through the Twelve Steps.*
12. *Alcoholics Anonymous.*
13. J. L. Kellermann, *Alcoholism, A Merry-Go-Round Named Denial* (Center City, Minn.: Hazelden Educational Materials, 1975).
14. *Alcoholics Anonymous.*
15. Ibid., 59.
16. *Practice guideline for the treatment of patients with nicotine dependence,* American Psychiatric Association (1996) 22.
17. The Twelve Steps of Alcoholics Anonymous reprinted with the permission of Alcoholics Anonymous World Services. Permission to reprint and adapt the Twelve Steps does not mean that AA has reviewed or approved the contents of this publication, nor that AA agrees with the views expressed herein. AA is the program of recovery from alcoholism. Use of the Twelve Steps and Twelve Traditions in connection with programs and activities are patterned after AA but which address other problems does not imply otherwise. The Twelve Steps of AA are:

1. We admitted we were powerless over alcohol—that our lives had become unmanageable.
2. Came to believe that a Power greater than ourselves could restore us to sanity.
3. Made a decision to turn our will and our lives over to the care of God *as we understood Him.*
4. Made a searching and fearless moral inventory of ourselves.
5. Admitted to God, to ourselves, and to another human being the exact nature of our wrongs.

6. Were entirely ready to have God remove all these defects of character.
7. Humbly asked Him to remove our shortcomings.
8. Made a list of all persons we had harmed, and became willing to make amends to them all.
9. Made direct amends to such people wherever possible, except when to do so would injure them or others.
10. Continued to take personal inventory and when we were wrong promptly admitted it.
11. Sought through prayer and meditation to improve our conscious contact with God *as we understood Him*, praying only for knowledge of His will for us and the power to carry that out.
12. Having had a spiritual awakening as the result of these steps, we tried to carry this message to alcoholics, and to practice these principles in all our affairs.

18. *Touchstones; Each Day a New Beginning;* Casey, *If Only I Could Quit;* Chandler, *Gentle Reminders*.
19. See also "Freedom from bondage" in *Alcoholics Anonymous*, 3rd ed. (New York: Alcoholics Anonymous World Services, 1976), 544–53.
20. "Some steps for recovery and empowerment," by Charlotte Kasl, which is included in her book *Many Roads, One Journey,* published by HarperCollins, 1991. These steps are reprinted by permission of the author.

Appendixes

1. Reprinted with permission of Nicotine Anonymous World Services.
2. Ibid.
3. Ibid.
4. The Preamble reprinted with permission of the AA *Grapevine*.
5. How It Works reprinted and adapted with permission of Alcoholics Anonymous World Services Inc.
6. Twelve Steps reprinted for adaptation with permission of Alcoholics Anonymous World Services Inc.
7. The Twelve Traditions of Alcoholics Anonymous reprinted with the permission of Alcoholics Anonymous World Services. Permission to reprint and adapt the Twelve Traditions does not mean that AA has reviewed or approved the contents of this publication, nor that AA.agrees with the views expressed herein. AA is a program of recovery from alcoholism. Use of the Twelve Steps and Twelve Traditions in connection with programs and activities patterned after AA but which address other problems does not imply otherwise. The Twelve Traditions of AA are

1. Our common welfare should come first; personal recovery depends upon AA unity.

2. For our group purpose there is but one ultimate authority—a loving God as He may express Himself in our group conscience. Our leaders are but trusted servants; they do not govern.

3. The only requirement for AA membership is a desire to stop drinking.

4. Each group should be autonomous except in matters affecting other groups or AA as a whole.

5. Each group has but one primary purpose—to carry its message to the alcoholic who still suffers.

6. An AA group ought never endorse, finance, or lend the AA name to any related facility or outside enterprise, lest problems of money, property, and prestige divert us from our primary purpose.

7. Every AA group ought to be fully self-supporting, declining outside contributions.

8. Alcoholics Anonymous should remain forever nonprofessional, but our service centers may employ special workers.

9. AA, as such, ought never be organized; but we may create service boards or committees directly responsible to those they serve.

10. Alcoholics Anonymous has no opinion on outside issues; hence the AA name ought never be drawn into public controversy.

11. Our public relations policy is based on attraction rather than promotion; we need always maintain personal anonymity at the level of press, radio, and films.

12. Anonymity is the spiritual foundation of all our Traditions, ever reminding us to place principles before personalities.

Hazelden Foundation, a national nonprofit organization founded in 1949, helps people reclaim their lives from the disease of addiction. Built on decades of knowledge and experience, Hazelden's comprehensive approach to addiction addresses the full range of individual, family, and professional needs, including addiction treatment and continuing care services for youth and adults, publishing, research, higher learning, public education, and advocacy.

A life of recovery is lived "one day at a time." Hazelden publications, both educational and inspirational, support and strengthen lifelong recovery. In 1954, Hazelden published *Twenty-Four Hours a Day,* the first daily meditation book for recovering alcoholics, and Hazelden continues to publish works to inspire and guide individuals in treatment and recovery, and their loved ones. Professionals who work to prevent and treat addiction also turn to Hazelden for evidence-based curricula, informational materials, and videos for use in schools, treatment programs, and correctional programs.

Through published works, Hazelden extends the reach of hope, encouragement, help, and support to individuals, families, and communities affected by addiction and related issues.

For questions about Hazelden publications,
please call **800-328-9000**
or visit us online at **hazelden.org/bookstore.**